DEALING WITH DEPRESSION

Jan Marsh recently retired after 40 years' experience as a clinical psychologist. During her career she worked in a variety of settings, including rehabilitation, mental health services, child protection, tutoring and court work. Most recently, she worked in private practice, focusing on adults who presented with anxiety, depression and challenging life issues.

DEALING WITH DEPRESSION

Simple ways to get your life back

JAN MARSH, M.A. (HONS), DIP.CLIN.PSYCH.

Empower

practical self-help tools by leading experts

First published 2016
This edition published 2019

Exisle Publishing Pty Ltd
PO Box 864, Chatswood, NSW 2057, Australia
226 High Street, Dunedin 9016, New Zealand
www.exislepublishing.com

A CiP record for this book is available from the
National Library of Australia.

ISBN 978-1-925335-93-4

Designed by Big Cat Design
Typeset in Miller Text 9.5 on 14pt
Printed by The SOS Print + Media Group (Aust) Pty Ltd

This book uses paper sourced under ISO 14001
guidelines from well-managed forests and other
controlled sources.

10 9 8 7 6 5 4 3 2 1

To the many clients over the years
who have taught me so much.

Disclaimer

The case studies in this book do not represent particular individuals but are composites from the author's years of clinical experience. Any resemblance to actual people is coincidental.

This book is a general guide only and should never be a substitute for the skill, knowledge and experience of a qualified professional dealing with the facts, circumstances and symptoms of a particular case. The nutritional, medical and health information presented in this book is based on the research, training and professional experience of the author, and is true and complete to the best of their knowledge. However, this book is intended only as an informative guide; it is not intended to replace or countermand the advice given by the reader's personal physician. Because each person and situation is unique, the author and the publisher urge the reader to check with a qualified healthcare professional before using any procedure where there is a question as to its appropriateness. The author, publisher and their distributors are not responsible for any adverse effects or consequences resulting from the use of the information in this book. It is the responsibility of the reader to consult a physician or other qualified healthcare professional regarding their personal care. This book contains references to products that may not be available everywhere. The intent of the information provided is to be helpful; however, there is no guarantee of results associated with the information provided. Use of drug brand names is for educational purposes only and does not imply endorsement.

CONTENTS

INTRODUCTION

From birth we are primed for growth and mastery. Watch a baby gain the most basic skills of survival and you will see the strength of that drive: to learn, to explore, to develop even the simplest skills, such as feeding from a bottle or a spoon or grasping an object. As the child grows, so does the drive to develop increasingly complex skills such as playing a sport, doing mathematics or learning a musical instrument. Children show us the pleasure of mastering a new skill and often, if they have some control over the process, they will persist for long periods of time. With every step of every skill the child asserts, 'This is my life and I can be effective in it.' We are designed for this: to learn and grow, and feel some sense of control in our lives.

When the fog of depression settles in, your familiar, capable way of life seems lost to you. It becomes hard to feel at all effective. But through good self-care and patience you can take back your life.

For those suffering from depression and those who are close to them, this book offers practical steps for a way forward.

Throughout this book I share some simple ideas to help you regain control of your life and push back depression. Most of these suggestions can be done at home or in your community at little financial cost. Some will deepen your relationships and help you find joy in daily life. That might sound like a bold claim, but when you take control you can improve your life.

Throughout my many years of work as a psychologist, I have noticed that when people are bogged down in how bad they feel and how badly they feel they are being treated — by life, their family, their workplace — they lose sight of simple things like a healthy diet, exercise, fun. When talking with clients I often found myself covering the basics of good self-care that form a strong foundation for wellbeing, no matter what issues or symptoms the client might bring. There is also the mental side of wellbeing. So many of us get around feeling not good enough, failing to notice all the day-to-day gifts life has to offer and unable to make meaningful contact with others for fear of being judged. Often those judgments are in our own minds. I believe that your mind, given the right conditions — including good self-care and supportive relationships — knows how to heal itself. By deciding to tune in to what you need and committing to some practical steps, you can make a difference to how you feel.

HOW TO USE THIS BOOK

There are two parts to this book. In Part 1, I give some background to depression, so that you can understand it and know what you're dealing with. My intention in this section is to demystify depression and remove any sense of shame attached to it. Depression is a process that follows the laws of nature and is no more shameful than catching the flu. I show how depression is diagnosed and how the symptoms affect body, mind and emotions. I also describe some causes of depression as well as some ways in which it may serve a purpose, for example, by highlighting the need for love in our lives or indicating when it's time to give up a course of action that's not paying off.

In Part 2, I share specific tips to improve your wellbeing in body, mind and spirit. It is a prescription for physical, mental and spiritual fitness that can go a long way towards both preventing and managing depression. I look at how you can take care of yourself and your connection to the world and to other people, and also how to cultivate attitudes that improve your resilience to the ups and downs of life.

If you are someone who likes to really understand a subject, read through Part 1 and get to know what depression is about. It will make the subject more approachable and give a rationale for the suggestions that follow in Part 2. I hope you will be able to see how the theory and practice are linked. Understanding how it all works will help you to find the motivation to do something to improve the way you are feeling.

If you are suffering and feel impatient to get on with doing something about it, you could turn straight to Part 2. You won't need to tackle all the tips, but I suggest you look at something from each of the three areas: body, mind and spirit. Pick one or two from each section and start with something that seems approachable. Depression eats away at motivation or immobilizes you with indecision, so make it as easy for yourself as you can. The important thing is to do something.

To counter depression you need to regain control of your life and a few successes, however small, will help you to feel effective. You will need whatever determination you can gather in order to make a start, but once you get into a routine and start to feel the benefits, motivation will follow. If you can do nothing else, go for a short walk, breathe deeply and slowly, emphasizing your exhalations, and look at your surroundings with open attention.

If you are not sure where to start, turn to 'Key points to remember' on page 161, glance down the list of tips and pick one action. Commit to it daily for a week and see what happens. The key points also offer a quick reference if you are having a dark day and need a tip to ease the pain. Look through the lists and choose something that is easy to implement in the present moment.

What I have written might seem very simple, in fact I hope it does. It might seem as though you know all this already — and you probably do, because deep down we know what we need. I want to refresh your memory and encourage you to commit to good practices that will give you back your life.

If you are supporting someone through depression, many of these suggestions, such as getting some exercise or healthy eating, can be implemented together and the tips are useful for a healthy life, whatever your circumstances.

When fog hides the blue sky, we know that the sky is still there, the fog will pass. Depression is like the fog and hope tells us there will be blue-sky days again.

PART 1

UNDERSTANDING

DEPRESSION

1.

WHAT IS GOING ON?

You wake at four in the morning and stare into the darkness, thinking of all the things that are wrong with your life and the world. You feel certain that it has always been so and the times you thought otherwise you were fooling yourself.

Just as it starts to get light you doze off and when the alarm rings you surface with difficulty from a blank, unrefreshing sleep.

Then you might do one of the following:

- Pull the blankets over your head and stay in bed until midday, when you get up, watch the soaps without remembering anything about them and forget to eat.
- Drag yourself out to face the day, put on a brave face at work and hope no one notices how often you go to the toilets to cry.
- Appear in the kitchen in your pyjamas, shout at the family and, when everyone is upset, throw on some clothes and storm off.
- Get up and drive around until the pub opens, then settle in to drink yourself numb.

You ask: What's the matter with me? Is it just me?

This could be depression and, no, it's not just you.

Depression is not something that happens to people who are weak or crazy. It is everywhere and it can affect anyone.

Scientists talk about a worldwide epidemic of depression. Often referred to as 'the common cold of emotional problems', depression is the subject of much study and concern. One in seven people will suffer from an episode of depression in their lifetime, and for women the rate is higher, up to one in five, although accurate figures are hard to establish due to variations in different cultures and age groups. Rates of depression are calculated by interviewing people from large random samples and establishing the level of their mood by using standard questions.

The reason for the gender difference in depression rates reported to such interviewers is not clear. Perhaps women are more ready to acknowledge feelings of hopelessness and self-criticism, while men mask their depression with other problems such as alcohol abuse and anger. Only about half of those who experience depression seek help, even though after an initial episode the chance of a recurrence is high.

The cost to society in terms of loss of productive work, damage to relationships and the effect on families is considerable. Depression is the leading cause of suicide, which is why it is so important to recognize and treat it promptly.

Let's meet some people who have come to terms with depression. We will get to know them throughout the book as they make changes in order to manage their low mood and improve their lives.

Laura, aged 32

I was brought up in a strict, religious family. We went to church every Sunday and had Bible study during the week. I was a timid child and I was sure that God was watching and finding fault with me all the time. My mother certainly was. She had a terrible temper and would beat my brother and me with a wooden paddle for the slightest offence. As well, she would say that we made God unhappy. I tried very hard but I could never please her. I loved my father, but he seemed scared of her too and didn't stand up for us.

I was a nerdy teenager who wore dowdy clothes and wasn't allowed to go to parties or dances. I had friends at school but because I couldn't socialize with them after school they weren't close friends.

When I left home to go to university I was a fish out of water. I had no idea how to mix with the other students, so I studied all the time. I think my first period of depression was caused by loneliness and overwork. I went to the Student Health doctor complaining of tiredness and she seemed to pick up that I was depressed, and she just advised me not to stay in bed and to have a routine for my study. I made a timetable that involved even more study, and I soldiered on.

Around that time I lost my faith and started drinking quite a lot. At first that helped a bit because I took time off from my books and I learnt to let my hair down. But the alcohol had a bad effect on me and some days I felt very black. In the end I seemed to get things into balance for myself. I finished my studies, though my grades weren't as good as they might have been, and I got a job that I enjoyed. I made friends through work and had more free time, so things were good for a few years.

Then I met Dave. We went out for a couple of years, and we got married when I was 26. I was happy when I became pregnant with Josh but the birth was a difficult one, and looking back I think I was quite traumatized. I knew I loved Josh but I just couldn't feel any pleasure in looking after him and I was so tired all the time.

It came to a head when I couldn't face any of the chores around the house and I was often still in my pyjamas at three in the afternoon. I took care of Josh, but that was all I could do. Dave would come home and cook the evening meal and put the washing on. I'd be back in bed by eight o'clock, often crying myself to sleep.

Jackson, aged seventeen

I never felt as good as other boys, even my brother. Especially my brother. He was such a star — good grades at school, captain of the winning football team, and he went out with the most beautiful girl.

High school became a real pressure because teachers expected me to be like him. It got worse as my mates became really keen to find girls to date and talked a lot about who they liked and how to ask them out. It wasn't so bad in my junior years but it did make me feel a dork not really having anything to say. I hung out for a while with the misfits but I hated the way they were so down on everyone, making really nasty comments and calling people 'gay' to put them down. I wondered what they said about me behind my back.

By Year 12 I worried a lot about what people thought of me, so I kept to myself. I started going to the library in the school breaks. After a while even the misfits stopped asking me to do things after school and nobody messaged me on the weekends, so I felt even worse.

My brother went to uni, so I was home on my own a lot for the last two years of school. Mum and Dad were working long hours and they went out together for bike rides and dinner on the weekends. They liked to have a drink, so there was quite a stash of alcohol in the kitchen cupboard. I picked a bottle of vodka because I could top it up with water and I had a few drinks when I was feeling down. It really helped. Soon I finished that one and used my pocket money to buy another one, and another one. I used my brother's ID, so it was easy. I left a half-finished bottle of mainly water in the cupboard and kept mine in my desk drawer. I'd have to smuggle the empties out in my school bag and down the road to someone's recycling bin on a Tuesday morning.

Funny, after a while the vodka didn't help any more. In fact, it made me miserable. I'd drink a bit and sit on my bed, looking at Facebook where my ex-friends were having a great time and I admit I'd cry.

Josie, aged fifteen

I went through a bad time when my parents split up when I was thirteen. I was angry with everyone and spent a lot of time in my room. My mum was sad all the time because it wasn't her idea to split and my dad was tied up with his new girlfriend and her four-year-old son, so no one really noticed me.

One of my friends told me it helped to cut yourself. I found a craft knife in the drawer and tried it on the top of my arm where it wouldn't show.

Somehow, when I was sad and hated my family for what they were doing, it helped to see the blood and afterwards I'd feel calm and kind of purified. Eventually my mother found out and she was horrified.

Tom, aged 58

I had a pretty successful engineering business that I built up from my dad's backyard operation. I worked long hours and probably didn't see as much of the family as I should have, but I really enjoyed the work and I was happy with the way I grew the business. I hadn't been university material or anything like that, but I had a knack and it went well.

My wife Sally was at me to slow down a bit and that seemed fair enough. Some of my mates had heart problems and they were only my age, so I saw it as a bit of a warning. When a bigger company made me an offer for the business I thought, why not? We could invest the money and live comfortably off it. The house was paid off, even the renovations, and we had new cars and the holiday house (which I hardly ever got to use) and the boat. I thought, Great, I'll retire early, do some fishing, visit the kids and spend time with the grandchildren.

So I sold the business for a good price, and they kept me on for a week or so to train the new manager. Then one day I woke up and didn't have to go to work. It was fine for the first week but then I started getting under Sally's feet. I'd had no idea what a busy life she led. I thought she would be around for company, but it was Monday painting class, Tuesday coffee morning, Wednesday gym and so on. She let me come to the gym with her but the other things were her time.

I can't say I even went through a stage of being bored. I just fell right into this black hole where I felt my life was over, no one needed me and somehow I'd got it all wrong. I started dwelling on all the things I wished I'd done differently. I wished I'd gone backpacking through South America. I thought of my first girlfriend and wondered whether I should have married her instead of Sally — I even looked her up online but I didn't contact her. I spent my days mulling over regrets and started planning how to do away with myself so that it would look like an accident. I even went down to the holiday house and took the boat out. I thought I could just slip over the side, but I was too scared to do it.

Then I was on the phone to my daughter and burst into tears.

Kathy, aged 45

I always felt that my parents treated me differently from my brothers and sisters. It seemed that there was never enough to go round and it was always me who missed out. I was quiet and tried not to be a nuisance but it didn't get me any better liked.

I went through life like that and was often the victim at work. I'd get dumped on and end up doing someone else's job or I'd be bullied and criticized by the boss. I changed jobs a lot but it always seemed to happen. My first husband was a bully too, but I took the children and left him; he seemed to respect me more after that and we got on okay as we raised the children.

My second husband is lovely, very generous and sensitive, and I could tell right away that we were meant for each other. It was fine for a while, but he lost his job and got very down and somehow the two of us got more and more depressed together. I thought I had some kind of illness and I kept going back to my doctor for tests but nothing ever showed up.

Each of these people has come to experience depression in a different way: Laura has been overwhelmed by becoming a mother, Jackson is in the shadow of his successful older brother and is unsure of his identity, Josie feels abandoned because her parents have separated, Tom has lost his role in life through retiring and Kathy has a long-standing feeling of malaise. The next few chapters will throw some light on how these different experiences can lead to depression.

2.

WHAT IS DEPRESSION?

Everyone feels 'down' or miserable at times, especially in the face of disappointment or loss. It may be because a relationship breaks up, or when someone we care about dies or moves away. It may be that we didn't get the job we hoped for or the situation we find ourselves in has become overwhelming and too hard to cope with. Most times, these feelings pass and we move on in some way. Gradually we take pleasure in the enjoyable aspects of our life again and the bad feelings fade.

However, if it's impossible to shake off the feelings of gloom and misery, even when something good happens, this might be the beginning of depression. People talk about the world looking grey and colourless, about the long dark night of the soul, about a black cloud or a black dog. Feelings of despair, helplessness and lack of hope are part of it.

Both Josie and Tom experienced major losses, which triggered their depression. In Josie's case the way in which her parents split up meant that she felt she had lost them both. Her mother was preoccupied with her grief and her father with his new family. Unable to get either of them to listen to how she felt,

Josie resorted to non-verbal communication; cutting herself not only relieved the pain for a while, it became a message to her mother.

Tom never imagined that his retirement would feel like a loss. After all, he had done well, he chose the right time to sell the business and he had the fruits of his hard work — the holiday house, the boat — right there to enjoy. But when it came down to it, his view of himself as a worker and an achiever took a severe blow and he needed help to adjust to the change in his life. This is a case where something that is mainly a positive change can still be experienced as loss and can lead to depression. Loss of self-image is a particularly hard thing to adjust to.

For Laura and Kathy, their family backgrounds contributed to their tendency to experience depression. In Laura's case, she found ways to cope with her emotions until the extra stresses and changes of having a baby triggered a full-blown postnatal depression. Kathy struggled with a long-term depression that seemed biological in nature and in spite of her best efforts was only lifted by medication.

As depression worsens, you might find it so hard to get motivated that even getting out of bed is a major effort. When you reach your limit, mind and body shut down and the simplest action becomes a major challenge.

Depression is not a sign of weakness. It is a common condition that can become serious. It can occur at any age and can be preceded by periods of anxiety and fear.

The good news is that depressive episodes can be treated, and even if they remain untreated most depressions are self-limiting; that is, they improve in time, usually in a matter of months.

With treatment, you can expect to make a full recovery. About half of those who have one episode of depression have another at some point in their lives, but often the second episode is recognized more quickly and help is found before it becomes too entrenched. By developing a good understanding of yourself and the particular triggers for depression that affect you, you can use a range of skills to lift yourself out of a down period before it becomes entrenched. With good self-care, depression can be prevented.

AM I DEPRESSED?

No one can give a full explanation of the causes of depression. There is no definitive test for it, such as a blood test or scan, but a familiar pattern does emerge, and there are four levels at which depression occurs.

In thoughts:
- inability to make decisions
- slower thinking
- lack of concentration
- poor memory
- thoughts of death or suicide plans
- expecting the worst.

In the body:
- lack of appetite or increased comfort eating leading to weight change
- sleep disturbances, especially waking early or sleeping too much
- loss of interest in sex
- lack of energy.

In the emotions:

- feelings of sadness or emptiness
- feelings of hopelessness and despair
- feelings of worthlessness or guilt
- crying more than usual, or becoming too numb to cry
- loss of pleasure in the things that used to be enjoyable.

In behaviour:

- avoidance — of other people, or of situations that might cause stress
- avoidance of formerly enjoyable activities
- passivity, lack of initiative or motivation
- loss of the usual range of behaviour in many areas of life.

Depression is identified first by its timeframe — has the depressed mood or loss of interest in the usual details of life lasted for at least two weeks and for most of each day? Secondly, there is a checklist of symptoms based on the pattern described above:

- depressed mood
- loss of interest and pleasure
- disturbance in appetite
- changes in sleep
- changes in activity level
- fatigue
- continual feelings of guilt
- difficulty in concentration
- thoughts or plans of suicide.

If five or more of these are present, depression is diagnosed. You can take a test online at cesd-r.com or www.depression.

org.nz. These are only guidelines to give you an idea of where to start. If you have concerns, see your family doctor or another health professional to talk about your situation and get a more accurate diagnosis.

SUICIDE

Suicide is the ultimate avoidance, a way out of the pain and despair that a depressed person is feeling. Many people, when saved from a suicide attempt, go on to have contented and successful lives, which makes a completed suicide an even greater tragedy. Since most depressions will improve in around three months, even if they are not treated, it is important for the depressed person to be kept safe from suicide and supported while they wait it out.

For this reason, if you know someone who is suicidal, or if you yourself have thoughts of ending your life, contact a doctor or mental health service for help to stay safe.

People might not openly talk about their thoughts of suicide, even if asked directly, but they might drop hints or show signs of putting their affairs in order. Close friends or relatives may become aware of changes in the person's behaviour that suggest they do not expect to be around for some future event. If so, it is important to let the doctor or someone who can care for that person know your concerns. If you can, it is good to get the permission of the person concerned but it is not necessary, as privacy must take second place to safety where there is a threat to the life or health of anyone.

It is not true that a person who talks about suicide will not do it. While some people have committed suicide without giving a hint of it to those around them, most do voice their ideas. Take them seriously.

If you are wondering whether you can survive the way you feel or are having thoughts of ending your life, this book is not for you yet. First seek professional treatment from a doctor or psychologist and, when you are on firmer ground, the actions I suggest in Part 2 will help you develop your skills and strengths to become truly well and resilient.

Developing an understanding of what depression is and how it affects you or someone close to you will provide a great base from which to create your own self-care package. Knowledge is power and will help you to take the first small steps out of the fog.

Let's take a look at what Laura, Jackson, Josie, Tom and Kathy did as their first steps towards taking back control.

Laura

After two weeks of feeling tearful and helpless, Dave insisted that I see the doctor. He even offered to come with me, but I didn't want him to know how bad I was really feeling. The doctor said I had postnatal depression and she wanted me to take antidepressants. I wasn't keen on that because I was breastfeeding, so she put me in touch with a postnatal depression support group. I went to meetings at the home of a woman named Maria, who had had PND and recovered. About six of us would bring our babies and have a cup of tea and talk.

On top of everything, I had been feeling sad that my mother wasn't the grandmotherly type who would come and help with the baby, and anyway I wouldn't have wanted her strict attitudes imposed on my child. It helped to find out that other women had to cope without their mums for various reasons. I didn't get better all at once, but talking did help and after a while we took our babies to a play group and just kept in touch in a friendly way. The other women encouraged me to talk to Dave about how I was feeling, and I found he could understand me pretty well. He didn't expect me to be superwoman.

Jackson

One morning Mum offered me a ride to school. I wanted to walk because I had two empties to get rid of, but she was in a motherly mood, so she insisted. When I got in the car there was a definite clink and Mum demanded to look in my bag. I got angry, but I had to let her. She looked so hurt I felt really bad. She dropped me off at school, taking the bottles and I just knew we'd have to talk about it 'when Dad got home'. I couldn't concentrate all day and I put off going home as long as I could, but there's only so much procrastinating you can do, walking the streets with no mates to hang out with.

Dad's a social worker, so he took it hard; you'd think underage drinking was the road to heroin trafficking and certain jail. I got angry again and said, 'What am I supposed to do when you're out all the time and I've got no mates?' I thought Mum was going to cry and I tried to leave the room, but Dad did his social-worker thing and made me sit down while he asked all these personal questions. I clammed up, but finally Mum came out with, 'Jackson, are you gay?' I shouted, 'No!' and stormed out.

Dad got me an appointment with someone he knew who did drug and alcohol counselling. She didn't seem very impressed with the really minor amount I was drinking, but she didn't like the fact that I was drinking it at home alone. I thought she'd just tell Dad it wasn't a problem, but she got on to the 'gay' thing too. I wanted to storm out again but instead I asked what I truly wanted to know: how would I tell? I was terrified to hang out with anyone my age, male or female. So, how would I know?

She looked at me for a while and then said it was okay not to know but if I wanted to 'explore' I could contact this Rainbow Youth organization. She gave me a card about them. It sounded, well, gay, but I took the card and tried to look as though she'd helped.

Josie

When Mum found out that I was cutting myself, she made me come to the school counsellor with her and we talked about what was going on. The counsellor got my dad to come in and she asked him to make a regular time to see me; it was a hassle because I had netball on the weekends, but we tried it for a while and he would come and watch my game and then take me for a hamburger afterwards. He didn't really know how to talk to me at first and I wasn't going to help him out till I saw whether he was going to stick to it. But he came every Saturday all winter, so it got better. I only cut myself again once when I called him and his girlfriend answered the phone, but then he made me meet her and she was okay I guess, so I just had to get over that. I don't really forgive him for making my mum so unhappy, but I have to admit he's trying his best with me. These days we just meet when it suits because I'm quite busy, but I know I can just phone up and make a time and if he hasn't heard from me he will call after a while.

Tom

My daughter was shocked when I got upset on the phone to her. I don't think she'd ever seen me cry. She said I better see the doctor, which I did and he gave me a referral to a psychologist. It all made so much more sense when I talked it through. I'm on Prozac, but it has been more important to plan some kind of life for myself. I was probably burnt out when I sold the business, but I need to work, I'm too young to retire, so I got a job in a plant nursery. I could buy and sell them ten times over but I'm working for wages and that's okay till I find out what I really want to do. I can take Sally out to dinner and the movies, things that I never had time for before, and we go to the holiday house most weekends. She even comes fishing sometimes.

Kathy

In the end the doctor referred me to the mental health service. I was reluctant because I've always been very private and independent, but the psychiatrist I saw was quite approachable. He explained how depression works, and when I thought about it I had to agree that I had probably been depressed on and off for most of my life. He suggested medication, but I didn't want to take pills, so he referred me to a psychotherapist.

The therapist talked about attachment and the 'fit'

between parents and child. That made a lot of sense to me because I am different from my boisterous brothers and sisters — maybe my parents just didn't know how to take that and let me get lost in the crowd. I learnt to be more assertive, but I still felt very down and would wake up in the early hours of the morning wishing I'd just died in my sleep. In a way it made it worse that I knew so much more and was trying to be different but was still so depressed. My husband found it hard too.

Finally I cried all through my therapy session and I had to agree that it would be worth trying medication. So, I took what the psychiatrist had suggested and in two weeks I felt completely different. It was as if the colours had all been switched on. I couldn't believe how easy life became without that weight dragging me down. Now I accept that I might need medication all my life and although it is good to learn to understand myself and gain new skills, those things alone won't help if the brain chemistry isn't right.

3.

WHAT CAUSES DEPRESSION?

Is depression a disease, like cancer, that should be treated and eradicated? Or is it like nausea, a signal to look at what is behind it and deal with that? It could be that depression is a symptom, just as a cough is, of a variety of problems. As in so many complex situations, the answer seems to be sometimes the former, sometimes the latter, sometimes a bit of both. There are many different ways to become depressed.

What seems to happen is a complex interaction between the inner world and the outer world. A combination of genes, brain chemistry, and your physical reaction to stress interacts with the events of the outside world and the environment in which you live your life. This is further shaped by your attitudes and beliefs, how you interpret the world around you and your place in it. Close relationships can protect you from depression but can also be damaged by the effects of depression.

GENES

Depression does run in families, which suggests that genes are involved. However, it is not a single gene disorder, like

Huntington's disease for example, where the presence of one gene means the individual will get the condition.[1] There are several 'susceptibility genes' for depression. This means that a tendency to become depressed runs in the family and can be triggered by certain circumstances. The lifetime study carried out at Otago University, Dunedin, New Zealand, which began in 1972 with the births of 1000 babies and has documented their lives regularly since then, showed that the researchers could pick out future depressives as early as age three, on the basis of temperament.[2] But it also showed that a good environment and a loving family can prevent full-blown depression from developing even if the genetic tendency is there.

Because of this interaction between genes and environment, different people become depressed in different ways. One might develop depression in spite of a life that is going well.

Another might react to a clear trigger, such as the death of someone close to them, and become depressed. Yet another could have a slight inherited susceptibility, keep it together during a stressful period such as a difficult job, then be tipped over by a bout of flu or a change of medication.

As with other illnesses that have a complex genetic pattern, the younger you are at the onset of the illness, the stronger the genetic factor. If you get further through life without being affected, the chances are it is environmental factors that bring on depression.

This has a bearing on some options for treatment, as we will see later in Chapter 9. If genetic and physical factors appear to be the strongest, medication will almost certainly be necessary. If the environmental factors predominate, psychotherapy and problem-solving skills may be the best approach.

BRAIN CHEMISTRY

There is a complex connection between the stress hormones such as cortisol and the balance of neurotransmitters in the brain. The pattern of noradrenaline, serotonin and dopamine affects mood but the mechanisms are not yet fully understood. Antidepressant medication is designed to act on these brain chemicals.

By doing MRI scans on depressed people, researchers have noticed that the blood flow to the prefrontal lobes of the brain — the area involved in thinking, planning and decision-making — is reduced during periods of depression and increases again after treatment.

Other areas of the brain that affect the balance between thought and emotional response are also affected. Researchers talk about the HPA axis, the fine balance between the hypothalamus and the pituitary in the brain and the adrenals in the body. Chemical information flows among these three and regulates the output of hormones.[3]

When the brain is flooded with the stress hormone cortisol, it becomes more vulnerable to damage from lack of oxygen. To protect the brain, it is important that depression is treated and relapses prevented as far as possible.

DAY-TO-DAY STRESS

A certain amount of stress in day-to-day life is not only inevitable, it can be a good thing, motivating and energizing us. But if there is too much stress, the system becomes overwhelmed, leading to feelings of anxiety and a desire to escape.

There is a link between anxiety and depression — biochemically, an over-stressed brain is more prone to depression. It may be that anxiety is the initial reaction to a difficult situation and depression comes about as the result of feeling helpless in the face of chronic anxiety.

The link between physical health and stress is generally accepted. We all know the stereotypes: the 'hyper' middle-manager with an ulcer or the overweight, overworking chain-smoker who is heading for a heart attack. But many others suffer the effects of chronic stress, either through their lifestyle or through personality type or both.

A detailed study of primates, who do not have addictions and bad diets to complicate the picture, shows that status contributes significantly to the hormones that affect health.[4] Dominant males have lower cortisol and higher 'good' cholesterol. Subordinate males have the opposite, resulting in poorer overall health. Females primates 'inherit' their status, so they do not have to fight their way to the top, but they still show the same pattern: high status means good health, low status leads to poorer health.

Depression could be likened to the defeat pattern used by mammals to signal that they are beaten and realize they have lost their position on the social ladder. When a vigorous young baboon makes a bid for the leadership of the troop he starts by fighting the male ranked directly above him. Baboons understand this ranking because it allows the male to fight all other males and mate with all the females below him. If he attempts something above his status he'll be threatened and if he persists there'll be a fight. It takes determination in a baboon to fight his way up through the ranks. Each time he's defeated he'll go away to lick his — actual — wounds and put himself on the sidelines for a while until his confidence recovers.

Of course, status in human society is not just about being the biggest and strongest and having the highest-status mate, though that can certainly come into it. Social status is much more complex and involves success on all kinds of levels depending on the values of the group you belong to or want to belong to. Money and material goods are taken as symbols of success in some groups but not in others. The mysterious code of teenage fashion, for example, dictates that the goods must be the right goods.

When ideas about status and stress are looked at in the workplace, it can be shown that a lack of control over your work, heavy demands from above and poor support create an environment that can change your body chemistry for the worse. Group dynamics are very important. A workplace that has good team spirit and a positive attitude is a healthy place to be. On the other hand, any bullying needs to be firmly dealt with before its toxic effects spread throughout the whole organization, sending stress levels rocketing.

Similar patterns can exist in families. The status–wellbeing connection is reflected in our health statistics, which show that income is related to health, partly because the wealthy can afford better health care, but also and significantly because poverty is stressful and carries low status, while those who are better off can feel comforted by their higher status.

CHILDHOOD EXPERIENCES

John Bowlby (1969) first alerted us to the need for a strong bond between parent and child, and many studies since have confirmed this.[5] Cases of children who are brought up in institutions, where their physical needs are met but they are not cuddled and talked to, can show us how important it is to have attachments to adult caregivers. Children who do not have this, go through a process of grief in which their protests give way to despair and they eventually give up trying to engage the attention of the people around them. They do not develop and learn as other children do and are more prone to depression later in life.

Lack of close attachment even affects the physical development of the brain, leading to reduced size and connectivity in some parts of the brain, particularly those that respond to and regulate emotions. On the other hand, securely attached infants more readily become independent and sociable. We are born to be loved. [6]

So, in addition to the basic needs of warmth, food, clothing and physical safety, every infant needs someone who is committed to caring for them. Caring parents tune in to their infants to help them learn about the world, their effectiveness in it and the trustworthiness of the important adults in their life. This will provide a secure base from which to go out and explore and to return for reassurance before venturing forth again. Without that stable bond, all the tasks of the growing child are much harder to achieve.

With good parenting and a positive environment, even a child with a vulnerable nature can be helped to develop confidence and learn the skills needed for life.

But for some, the events of childhood are traumatic and stresses later in life can trigger a reaction that involves past as well as present circumstances. For example, a woman whose mother died when she was a child may be overwhelmed with loss when her relationship breaks up. A young man whose parents ignored him might become intensely attached to his partner, perhaps to the point of being overly possessive and risking the very closeness he wants so much.

Some childhood experiences create a condition known as

learned helplessness. This is when the child learns that no matter what they do, they cannot change what will happen. This may become a pattern of negative thinking along the lines of, 'Nothing ever works out for me' or 'What I want doesn't matter'. This is particularly noticeable in people who have been beaten or sexually abused as children and feel powerless to change their life.

For Kathy, the way her parents treated her, by giving her less than her siblings, gave a clear message that she was somehow inferior. That, combined with her natural timidity and possibly a genetic tendency to depression, set the scene for a lifelong battle with low mood. While she could understand how this had happened, the changes in her brain chemistry meant that she could only get on top of it with the help of medication.

Even people who have had a happy childhood can become depressed. And each person's interpretation of their childhood is uniquely their own. To a child trying to make sense of the world and their role in life, seemingly innocent events can have a huge impact for better or for worse.

LOSS AND SHAME

Psychotherapists since the time of Freud have understood the connection between loss and depression.[7]

In susceptible people loss may trigger the 'defeat' pattern, which sets off a series of physical changes. Think of how your dog reacts when you tell him off: with ears down, tail between his legs, and lowered shoulders, his whole body tells you he submits. Or your cat, if she is regularly defeated by the neighbour's tom, neglects her grooming, loses interest in her food and refuses to go out to play. Humans also show signs of defeat, in body posture as well as mental attitude.

Some losses, particularly through death or the end of a close relationship, are obvious and the people around you will acknowledge what you are going through. This makes it easier to get a handle on the situation and your feelings. In the case of death, the funeral helps with the process of grieving and letting go and brings people together to support each other.

As Tom discovered, sometimes events might not be identified as losses. The grief may be triggered by the loss of a dream or an ideal, the loss of the image we have of ourselves or the beliefs we held dear. Sometimes it takes a skilled therapist to unravel your story and pinpoint the loss that is hidden inside it.

ATTITUDES AND BELIEFS

From their earliest years, people try to make sense of their environment. Everyone develops beliefs about themselves, other people and the world around them. Some of these go so deep that they are not put into words — they are simply regarded as absolute truths. Positive beliefs such as 'I am loved' or 'The world is a wonderful and exciting place' enhance the person's feelings of competence and pleasure in exploring the world. Beliefs that pave the way for depression could be 'I am useless' or 'Nobody cares about me'.

These fundamental beliefs or 'core beliefs' shape the way you see yourself and the world. They also shape a set of attitudes, expectations and assumptions that dictate your reactions, for example:

- Core belief: 'I am useless.'
- Attitude: 'It's terrible to be useless, people must hate me.'
- Expectation: 'I have to work harder than anyone else.'

- Assumption: 'If I work as hard as I possibly can I might be able to do some things and some people might like me a little.'

These beliefs trigger automatic thoughts. The constant chatter of our brain goes on, often at a level we barely notice, but the content of those automatic thoughts can have a powerful effect on mood. There is more on this subject in Chapter 6.

We can apply our knowledge of the causes of depression to the characters we have met. Through early experiences combined with genes that predispose her to depression, Kathy has struggled throughout life and we can assume there are changes in her brain chemistry that make it hard for her to have a positive mood even when things are going well. She is also vulnerable to being victimized at work because it mirrors how she feels about herself. Laura's strict religious upbringing set high standards that she worked hard to reach. Her core belief was 'I am not good enough'. Along with the high standards came a fear of failure and an inability to relax. She had to learn to pace herself and to have fun. Jackson is questioning his role in his social group, which is important for a teenager's sense of belonging, and is vulnerable to feeling he has low status. As well as experiencing grief about the loss of his work, Tom has lost his high status by retiring and is questioning his purpose. Josie's issue is one of attachment because her parents' separation has left her feeling isolated, with the suspicion that her mother is too busy for her and her father has more time for his new partner's little boy.

4.

DOES DEPRESSION
HAVE A PURPOSE?

It may seem strange to think that a condition as painful and debilitating as depression could have a purpose. The parallel with physical pain is helpful. Pain is necessary to our safety: it lets us know when something hot or sharp is causing damage, when an illness needs attention or when our body has been over-exerted and needs rest. Depression can be seen as a sign that all is not well emotionally and it can alert us to some potential harm or imbalance in life.

Below are some ways in which depression can serve a useful function. An explanation or understanding of the role of depression has been sought from earliest times to the present day.

EARLY EXPLANATIONS

At the time of Hippocrates (fifth century BC), the Greek doctor acknowledged as the founder of modern medicine, disease was thought to originate from an imbalance of bodily fluids. There were thought to be four fluids, called humours, which were associated with the elements of the earth as well as certain personality types and particular diseases. We still use some of the ancient terms, such as choler for anger and phlegmatic for a very calm, stable person. One of the humours, melancholia, is the origin of the term melancholic to mean depressive.

Later, during the Middle Ages, depression and all other forms of mental illness were thought to be caused by witchcraft and demonic possession. Treatment involved purging and exorcism and was more likely to be in the hands of religious leaders than doctors.

The role of the church declined as society became more secular and scientific. Medical science progressed rapidly in the nineteenth century and with this development came an understanding that some psychological problems were associated with brain disorders such as the effects of advanced syphilis. Depression came to be regarded as a sign of genetic deterioration in a family, which could be passed down through the generations, and a stigma developed.

Sigmund Freud, writing in the late nineteenth and early twentieth centuries, began with an interest in neurology but moved on to develop his theories of the psychological causes of mental illness. He became aware of the influence of life experiences on the individual and his treatment was based on the idea that drives and beliefs are held in the part of the mind that is mostly out of conscious awareness. He used techniques to help his patients become more aware of what motivated them and to learn to come to terms with certain experiences and patterns of behaviour and to make changes. Although the techniques of therapy have changed over the years, many of the underlying assumptions of modern thought can be traced to Freud and his colleagues.

Alfred Adler, a contemporary of Freud's, came closer to the modern understanding of depression when he examined the role and influence of inferiority complexes and social status on the individual.[1] He was interested in the way in which physical symptoms express emotional needs and difficulties and how they are overcome; for example, how a stutterer might overcompensate and become a great orator. Adler developed the concept of 'fictions', the working models we each develop as a child and use to guide our life, and his therapy encouraged the patient to take responsibility for an improved way of life.

WHAT IS THE PURPOSE OF DEPRESSION?

In a society that wants everything to be pleasant and easy, it may seem ridiculous to search for a purpose for something as distressing as depression. However, let's assume that it is there for a reason. There are a number of ways to look at the purpose of depression. Here are a few.

A warning

Perhaps, like physical pain, emotional pain serves as a warning. If you sprain your ankle, the pain reminds you not to walk on it until it has healed. If you over-ride the pain, you may cause more serious damage, whereas if you rest until you can walk with much less pain, healing will be well under way.

The rare person who does not experience physical pain lacks important information about danger and will have to consciously take care to avoid getting cut, burnt or otherwise harmed. Depression may have a similar warning function.

Depression may be telling us we are on the wrong track as far as our life's goals are concerned. Maybe we are trying to fit ourselves into a role that does not suit us, maybe we are bored and ready for a change but lack the courage to step off a safe path. If we do not make the best use of our skills and talents, depression may be the result. It may be warning us to follow our destiny and choose a path into which we can put our heart and soul.

It may also be a warning that the path we are on is overwhelming, such as in the current trend to overwork. When a person subjects themselves to continual pressure, sometimes the system simply shuts down.

A reminder of love

Evolutionary psychologists suggest that depression has evolved alongside our need to form close social relationships.[2] We are highly motivated to be wanted and valued and to hold status in relation to other people. Signals that we are getting these things make us happy. Information that we are not wanted or valued or that we have lost status can be one of the causes of depression. Depression is strongly marked by feeling distant and cut off from others.

So depression could be the other side of love. It reminds us to value close relationships and to seek them out and it gives us an opportunity to adjust to the loss of someone close. Some therapists suggest that depression is like a glimpse of death, allowing us to get used to the idea that loss is a part of life.

An end to the fight

Depression may also be telling us to stop fighting when the odds are against us. As we have seen, primates, and in fact most mammals, have a hierarchical system that depends on members fighting their way to the top. Most animals have a ritualized way of submitting that prevents the loser from being seriously damaged. We no longer fight to the death for our status (except in unusual circumstances), but day-to-day life involves a constant testing of where each person stands. Depression may be the way human beings withdraw from the field to prevent further harm.

The off switch

Depression might prevent us from wasting energy attempting the impossible. For a million years our ancestors kept the same way of life, using simple tools that did not change or improve, hunting the same species, living in the same places. Then homo sapiens came along. Tools evolved and became more varied and skillful, art appeared on cave walls and migrations set forth to spread out across the world. There is something in homo sapiens that causes us to strive for change and for achievement. Without an off switch we could burn ourselves out. Is depression the off switch?

Hibernation

Depression could also be telling us to get some rest. When daylight was the only source of light, human beings were active in the day and slept all night. With artificial lighting, we can be active at any time, day or night, and the use of computers and phones with their brightly lit screens can have a powerful effect on the brain's ability to establish a routine.

Although the complex relationship between the biological clock and depressive symptoms is far from being fully understood, research into the biochemistry of depression has shown that the circadian rhythm, which controls our pattern of wakefulness and sleep and keeps us in a day–night cycle, is disturbed in depressed subjects. Shift-workers are more prone to depression, as are women who experience disturbed sleep, through changes in hormones as in menopause or pregnancy or through attending to the needs of small children who wake in the night. Even the fathers of young babies can become postnatally depressed just as new mothers can, perhaps through lack of sleep.

Aspects of depression are similar to hibernation in that many body processes slow down, as they do in animals that hibernate. For those who experience depression during autumn and winter this can make sense.

Some antidepressant medications act on the hormones that regulate the circadian rhythm, correcting problems such as early-morning waking and oversleeping. Light therapy and sleep restriction can also re-set the biological clock.

Gestation

Just as the seed grows in the dark, important changes might need a period of down time to develop. Feeling 'stuck' or lacking in direction often characterizes the depressed state. But it could be that unconscious processes are at work below the surface. Out of depression may come a new direction in life, a creative idea or the recognition of the need to change in some significant way. Be patient. Rather than protesting about the down time, look at how you can use it to find your direction.

Spiritual regrouping

In spiritual writing, the concept of the 'dark night of the soul' is similar to depression. The loss of life energy, or libido, that is a part of depression causes the sufferer to withdraw from seeking answers in the outside world and to look within. In this view, depression takes away our pleasure in mundane activities and may be asking us to re-evaluate the way we understand our life.

Spirituality is both a sense of something beyond ourselves and a way of understanding important aspects of life and death, good and evil, beauty and awe. All human beings try to make sense of themselves and their environment in a continual search for meaning; coming to some spiritual understanding can be an important part of this.

For some, their spiritual needs are met by being members of a church and attending religious services. Others feel the presence of the divine in nature, and yet others find that the loving kindness of other human beings represents the qualities of a higher power or self. Creativity is another way to connect with something beyond ourselves, and many artists, musicians and writers feel that their work has an important spiritual aspect to it. Self-expression is also important in linking with the human community and feeling part of something beyond ourselves.

————

Seeking the purpose in a depressive episode is a way of finding out what this experience can communicate about your life. This will give you clues to the adjustments that will help you to recover and to take care of yourself to prevent a relapse. Take a few moments to ask yourself: 'What is depression trying to tell me?' You may be surprised at the way an answer makes itself felt. This will give you guidance as you tackle the next section and choose some changes that will enhance your life and help you overcome depression.

PART 2

TAKING CONTROL

5.

TAKE CARE
OF YOURSELF

Depression eats away at your feelings of being effective in the world, so when you start to tackle depression, your first task is to reclaim some control over your life. This doesn't have to be any great achievement, just a sense of being able to take care of the basic tasks. If depression has eroded your life until even getting up in the morning is a major challenge, then simply setting the alarm and dragging yourself into the shower will be a way of reasserting that you can be in charge of some part of your life, however small.

Part of good mental health is an awareness of yourself as a capable individual. People who have this self-concept take good care of themselves and are healthier and happier than those who don't.

Taking action, any action that is possible, can be a way to begin rolling back the depression.

FIRST — TAKE STOCK

Take stock of how you've been feeling and behaving lately. Ask yourself how you are doing in terms of the basics of a healthy life. Are you living up to what's best for you?

Have a look at the checklist in Chapter 2. Do some of these symptoms describe how you feel? This could indicate that you have depression. If so, try to accept it without worrying too much about how it came about or feeling ashamed of being depressed. Depression is a natural process, it affects a lot of people and it can be overcome. Remember that feelings of guilt or failure can be part of depression. In spite of such feelings, come to terms with where you are at and choose some steps that will help you to change things.

If depression has been around for a while, you might find it hard to identify the trigger for feeling down. Also, the way in which depression clouds your thinking will make that kind of exploration difficult. Start with acceptance — don't judge yourself and don't worry too much about 'why'.

The next step is to start looking after yourself. Depression can disrupt important basic functions such as eating and sleeping, and can also sap motivation, which makes other functions such as personal hygiene and social contact difficult. Start by taking care of basics. Don't ask whether you deserve it or whether you want to do it. Decide to make a start, give yourself at least a month of good self-care and then review it.

While you do this basic self-care program, shelve all the major questions such as 'What is the point of my life?' or 'Should I leave my marriage?' Stay with the here and now and work on the basics. This will take a little faith, but what have you got to lose? Depression feels pretty bad, so why not give yourself a chance to feel a little better? Treat it as an experiment in which you are going to find out what works for you.

It is a good idea to start with a thorough check-up from your GP. Physical conditions such as iron or vitamin deficiency, thyroid problems or a virus can lead to low mood and should be ruled out or treated.

Now to the basics.

FIVE EVERYDAY THINGS THAT CAN REDUCE DEPRESSION

1. Breathe

Breathing is an interesting function. To some extent it can be under conscious control but it also goes on automatically whether or not we are aware of it and whether we are awake or asleep. There are all kinds of ways to breathe, some of which really tax concentration and require mastery. You may have discovered this if you have ever attended yoga classes, which show you how to do certain breathing exercises.

Mainly, you should aim to make optimal use of the lungs by opening the chest and using the diaphragm so that body and brain become well oxygenated. This alone can give a sense of wellbeing, whereas poor oxygen intake gives a feeling of stress or even desperation.

Start with posture. Stand or sit tall and straight, then gently let your chest open so that the diaphragm can do its work. Let your spine stack up neatly, vertebra by vertebra, and your shoulder-blades relax down your back, with your head balanced lightly on your neck as if you were pointing the crown of your head to the sky.

This might be a challenge. Through feeling depressed, your

body may have adopted the defeat posture: shoulders hunched, head down as you shrink away from the world. Being tall and straight might feel a bit 'out there', even aggressive, if you are not used to it. Try it in front of a mirror and make sure you smile at yourself. You will see that it looks good: healthy and open but not confronting.

As you get used to a tall, open posture, the message will flow from your body to your brain, indicating that you are in control and all is well. Some people benefit greatly from this very simple step of straightening up. To maintain it you will need to check in often during the day and remember to stack, relax, and aim for the sky.

Your breathing will automatically improve with an open posture because it gives the diaphragm room to move, whereas slouching cuts it off, trapping it in the fold of the abdomen. The diaphragm is a large muscle lying horizontally below the lungs. When it moves downwards it draws in air like a bellows. If you put your hand on your stomach just below your ribs and breathe in, letting the air fill your lungs from the bottom, you should be able to feel your abdomen rise a little as your diaphragm moves downwards. When you release the breath, the diaphragm relaxes upwards, pressing the air out. These movements don't have to be very strong unless you are running hard or climbing a hill. Day to day, the diaphragm tirelessly works away for you. Now and again, check in to make sure you are giving it the space it needs.

Breathing is affected by the fight-or-flight response, a survival instinct that is about creating safety. We activate it when we believe there is a chance we can outrun or outfight our attackers. When we are stressed or anxious, the fight-or-flight response changes the breath to prepare for action, causing many people to breathe shallowly, using the small muscles between the ribs at the top of the chest. This is hard work for these little muscles and they become tired and strained, sometimes causing chest pain that mimics heart problems. In addition, a short, panting breath fails to fill the lungs, disturbing the balance between oxygen and carbon dioxide in the body, which may cause light-headedness or pins-and-needles in fingers and lips.

The freeze response, however, is activated when running or fighting is not an option and the best hope is to try to go unnoticed. In depression, this may be the response that is activated by giving up. The freeze response causes people to hold their breath, often for quite long periods of time. If you find yourself sighing or gasping in a long breath now and then, or running out of breath when you speak, you might be holding your breath and blocking the natural flow of air.

Either way, stressed breathing can feel quite frightening, but is easy to fix.

Breathe in through your nose. This warms and filters the air and helps to control the breath and form it into a steady flow. Breathe out through your nose or your mouth as you prefer. Try to breathe with your diaphragm. If you don't usually do this, it will feel strange. Some people experience a rush of emotion, even tears, at first. But after a while, if you can get used to the sensation, diaphragmatic breathing gives a feeling of confidence and wellbeing. You don't need a lot of air but you must breathe in fully, letting the air fill all of the available lung space. Let an even rhythm develop between the in-breath and the out-breath. As a guide, try counting to three as you breathe in and three out.

If it is hard to grasp the idea of better breathing, a physical therapist can help by showing how the muscles work and suggesting exercises to assist you. There are also some excellent sites on the internet.

BREATHING EXERCISES FOR RELAXATION

Turn your attention to your breathing. What's happening?

When we feel relaxed, we breathe slowly and deeply. By consciously making our breathing slow and deep, we can create a feeling of wellbeing and relaxation, sending the message to our brain that we are safe and well.

There are many breathing exercises to assist with this. Yoga instructors and physiotherapists are skilled in these and there are tips online. But this tool is available to everyone, anytime. You can tune in to your breathing and, with a bit of practice, create a powerful tool for feeling in control and relaxed.

Here are some suggestions.

1. Belly breathing

Sit or lie comfortably and put one hand on your abdomen, just below your ribs, and the other on your chest. You may feel the rise and fall of your breath even before doing anything conscious.

Take in a full breath through your nose, allowing the air to reach the bottom of your lungs. Your belly will push your hand outwards or upwards (depending on whether you are sitting or lying down). Try not to let your chest move.

Breathe out through your mouth, pursing your lips a little as if whistling. Feel your hand sink down as your lungs empty.

Do this slowly and mindfully up to ten times. Notice how you feel at the end of the exercise.

2. 4-7-8 breathing

This exercise also uses belly breathing, with the addition of timing your breaths by counting.

Start as above, seated or lying down, with one hand on your belly and one on your chest.

Breathe in slowly through your nose, counting silently to 4.

Hold your breath to the count of 7.

Breathe out to the count of 8. Control and pace your out-breath so that your lungs have emptied by the time you reach 8.

Repeat up to seven times, noticing how you feel. This exercise can be good for getting off to sleep.

3. Roll breathing

Again, start seated or lying down with one hand on your belly and one on your chest. Notice how your breath moves your hands.

First do belly breathing so that the hand on your belly rises and the hand on your chest remains still. Do a few cycles of this, breathing in through your nose and out through your mouth.

Now breathe in slowly and deeply so that your belly lifts your lower hand, and then continue breathing into your chest so that your other hand rises.

Breathe out with a gentle whooshing sound, letting first your belly, then let your chest sink. The movement as you breathe in and out like this is like rolling waves.

Practise for 2 to 5 minutes and notice how you feel.

Caution: some people feel a little dizzy or lightheaded when they first do breathing exercises. If this affects you, slow your breathing. Always get up slowly after breathing exercises.

4. Morning breath

This is a pleasant stretch way to start the day.

Stand with your feet hip-width apart. As you exhale, bend forward from the hips and let your arms dangle towards the floor.

Straighten up slowly, inhaling as you do so. Stand straight and gently hold your breath for a few seconds.

As you exhale, bend forward again and relax downwards.

Repeat three to five times. Don't force anything. Notice the feelings of relaxation.

2. Relax

Don't mistake the immobilization of depression for relaxation. You might have spent most of the afternoon stuck on the couch staring out the window, but if your muscles are tense and your mind is rehearsing every possible worst-case scenario, you certainly won't get up feeling refreshed.

Our muscles accumulate tension throughout the day and

don't release all that tension overnight when we sleep. It takes conscious attention to fully relax.

One way to do this is through progressive muscle relaxation, by tensing and relaxing each muscle group, taking about 15 minutes to work through the whole body. The idea behind this method is that muscles can recognize the contrast between actively tensing and then letting go and will continue to relax even after your attention moves on to the next muscle group. A relaxed body leads to a relaxed mind. [1]

Start by choosing somewhere comfortable to sit or lie down, at a time when you won't be disturbed. Turn off your phone and check that your clothing is loose and comfortable, and that you are not too hot or too cold. Take a few slow breaths: breathe in, hold for 1 or 2 seconds, then breathe out. Now turn your attention to one hand. Make a fist and notice the tension you have created. Hold to the count of five. Now release your hand and feel the relaxation flow into it. Allow that to develop for 10 or 15 seconds then repeat: make a fist, notice the sensation, release and let the relaxation develop. Continue throughout the body. You can tense your arm by drawing your hand up to your shoulder, or by stretching your arm out stiffly. You can tense your legs by pressing your heels down on the floor (or the bed if you are lying down), pointing your toes or turning them up towards your face. Your belly can be pulled in or pushed out. You will get the general idea. Try working through your body in this way. If your attention wanders, come back to the muscle group you are focusing on and notice the sensations you create as you tense and relax. There are instructions online for this type of relaxation, or you can record your own instructions on your phone or other device, either in your own voice or by asking a friend with a pleasant voice to talk you through them.

Different people relax in different ways. For some, audio instructions work well. There are various options: besides the method described above, some ask you to think your way through each part of the body, softening and relaxing each muscle group without adding any tension; some offer a guided visualization by describing a safe and relaxing place or activity such as walking on a beach or in a forest; others have soothing music.

Some people may be able to meditate, sitting quietly and emptying their mind of the constant chatter. This becomes easier when you understand that it is the brain's nature to be busy making connections. Rather than criticizing yourself for not being able to stop your thoughts, try to observe the thoughts calmly and give them a name: 'worrying', 'remembering', 'planning'. Some meditation teachers suggest thinking of thoughts as if they were clouds in the sky — the clouds come and go while the sky remains constant. Another helpful image is to think of thoughts like cars on a motorway: if you rushed out onto the road to try to stop them you would feel frantic and very unsafe, but if you stand at the side observing and naming them — 'Oh, there's a blue Toyota ... a yellow sedan ...' — you can relax.

Others find movement suits them better: yoga exercises, Tai Chi or a gentle walk can be helpful. The main thing is to focus on the activity without judgment, letting it take your full attention and so blocking out negative thoughts and feelings, and to do it in a way that does not put stress on the body.

Reading can also be an ideal way to switch off both mind and body and enter the world the writer has created. It may challenge your concentration at first because of the way depression affects concentration. It often helps to start with magazine articles or short stories and ideally aim for something light, humorous even.

'Active relaxers' need a bigger focus on activity and tend to appreciate a complex activity. Swimming or running might fill the need, or domestic activities such as cooking, housework or gardening, which can be done in a relaxing way. Focus on the activity itself without rushing it and set aside any judgment about the outcome. Doing one thing at a time without letting your mind race on to the next task can be very relaxing.

A common source of tension is driving. Often there is a need to be somewhere at a certain time and a sense of threat from other drivers, as well as being aware of the actions of driving in themselves, can pile on the stress. Try to find a sense of relaxation within the alertness. This will include trusting that most drivers stay in their lane and obey the rules, while being aware that we are all human and can make mistakes. Getting angry with other drivers won't change their behaviour and will make you feel stressed and upset, so keep calm and try to be as relaxed as possible.

Of course, listening to relaxation instructions or even relaxing music while driving would not be wise. However, there are some things you can do to make driving less stressful and even enjoyable. For a start, try to leave in plenty of time, allowing for busy times of day and choosing a good route, so that you're not anxious about delays in the traffic and can drive a little slower. This is less taxing on your skill and concentration.

You can make sure that your seat is as comfortable as possible — I added a firm cushion to mine — and the headrest and mirror are adjusted correctly so that your head is supported and your neck relaxed. You can use opportunities such as stopping at traffic lights to stretch and release your hands, arms and shoulders. Make sure you do a few stretches at the end of a long drive.

Another situation that is often far from relaxing is sitting at a desk or computer for much of your working day. While you concentrate on work and worry about deadlines and the demands of a job, your neck and shoulders tense up, causing headaches and a chronic sense of stress. Understanding this and dealing with it during the working day is really important — don't wait for your annual holiday to allow yourself to relax!

There are a number of websites that demonstrate or describe stretches to do at your desk. In particular, try some neck exercises, by tilting your head to the side so that your ear moves down to your shoulder, or turning your head to look over your shoulder. Hold the stretch for a few seconds and feel the relaxation as you turn back to the centre. Repeat a few times on each side. Arms and shoulders also respond well to stretches, either to the front or to the back by wrapping your arms around the back of the chair or grasping your elbows behind your back. A few twists using the back of the chair as leverage will do your back a world of good too! Of course, you can do these exercises wherever you are — you don't have to be at a desk. Take breaks and use opportunities such as hand-delivering something to have a short walk.

There are many ways to relax. The common thread is to feel safe and be in the present moment, focused on one thing (rather than many) as much as possible, and to allow the muscles of the body to soften while the chatter of the mind stills. A sense of safety can re-set the body's responses and convey an 'all's well' message to the brain. Research has found very tangible mental and physical benefits come from relaxation.[2]

Experiment and find out what helps you relax. A relaxed person will have soft muscles with no areas of soreness or tension, and improved blood flow, which creates warmth. If you have a suitable thermometer you could check this: hold the thermometer between finger and thumb while you do something that you find relaxing. See if your hand temperature increases.

Mental relaxation will become a rest from the worry and regret that can fill the depressed mind with negative ruminations. Being poised gently in the moment creates a sense of wellbeing that can be carried through the day.

Aim to spend 15 minutes every day in some form of relaxation.

3. Sleep

Depression can cause disturbances in the sleep pattern by either reducing or greatly increasing the amount of sleep. It is important to try to regulate your sleep pattern, partly to improve the quality of sleep and feeling of wellbeing and partly because disturbed sleep patterns can put you out of step with friends and family and make it hard to connect socially, get to work or take part in other activities on any sort of schedule.

Create a quiet, comfortable place to sleep that can be darkened completely with curtains or blinds to block out any street lights or early morning sun. Make sure you are warm enough; if necessary put on socks to keep your feet warm and have layered bedclothes that you can adjust according to the season.

Sleeping patterns and bedtime rituals

Now begin to establish a regular sleep pattern by getting up at the same time every morning. Set your alarm but be realistic by making changes in small steps. If you've been sleeping till midday, set the alarm for 10.30 or 11 am. If you've been waking at 5 am, set the alarm for 6 am. Without trying to change your time of going to sleep, start by getting up at a regular time.

Working back from your morning alarm, decide on an

appropriate bedtime. Again, be realistic. If you have only been getting five hours' sleep don't set out to make it eight straightaway. Try for six or so. If you have been sleeping for twelve hours at a stretch, try ten.

Aim to go to bed and wake up at the same time every day and don't allow yourself to nap during the day. But if you must nap, set an alarm or timer for half an hour. This has been shown to be enough time for a refreshing nap without getting into a deep sleep from which you will wake groggy.

Now set up a bedtime ritual. This might involve a hot drink (but no caffeine, of course), a relaxing bath or shower, changing into comfortable pyjamas and reading or listening to music for a few minutes before putting out the light. You can practise your breathing and relaxation exercises before going to sleep. Try to avoid using computers, phones or other screens for at least one hour prior to bedtime. Screens that emit blue light suppress the production of melatonin (the hormone that signals sleepiness to our brain) and can delay sleep onset. TV should be banned from the bedroom if possible. Working or watching TV in bed makes our brain associate bed with an active mind, making it harder to switch off.

Don't be too anxious if you don't get into a healthier sleep pattern right away. Expect to be more tired at first — this is good. Sleep is a natural process and sooner or later your brain will switch off and allow sleep to come. If at first you find you are awake for long periods of the night, get up and start your bedtime routine again with a hot drink, some relaxation exercises and so on.

Sleep-restriction therapy can be very helpful and involves reducing the total amount of time you spend in bed (but never to fewer than five hours). Initially, this controlled form of sleep restriction results in less sleep, but very soon you will find you get off to sleep more quickly and stay asleep throughout the night, so that you are getting shorter but better-quality sleep. As your sleep efficiency improves, gradually increase the amount of time you spend in bed, usually by 15 to 20 minutes each week, until your sleep/wake cycle gives you the best daytime alertness possible.

Food, drink and exercise to help with sleep

Pay attention to what you eat and drink. Nicotine, caffeine and alcohol all have a bad effect on sleep. Alcohol may make you sleepy at first but wakeful later in the night. Aim to be moderate with these substances or even abstain from them altogether while you sort out your sleep. Other recreational drugs and even some prescribed medications can interfere with sleep.

Going to bed too full or too hungry can also make it hard to get to sleep, so eat a light meal, not too late in the evening. Some foods aid sleep better than others, so think about having some protein with the evening meal and perhaps a milky drink. Sweet foods can give an energy boost, so be cautious about sugary food or drink in the evening. There is now evidence that people who eat high-fibre foods in the evening sleep better, so it might be worth considering adding chickpeas or other legumes, or whole grains such as oats and buckwheat, to your meal.[3]

Get some exercise every day (see page 62). Physical exercise makes it easier for you to fall asleep and to sleep more deeply. Some people find if they exercise in the evening they are energized and more wakeful. If this happens, make sure you are more active earlier in the day — try a walk or a swim at lunchtime.

Stress management

Whether you are in a paid job or caring for children at home, as far as possible structure your day in doable chunks. Be organized, prioritize and delegate. If there is too much to do, focus on the task at hand and be as present as you can. At the end of the day make a note of what you've achieved and write a to-do list for the next day. Then put it aside. If you wake in the night worrying about work, keep a pen and paper by the bed and make a note of your concern. If it pops back into your mind, say to yourself, 'I've made a note, I'll look into it tomorrow'. There's not much that needs to be attended to at two in the morning. If you are persistently kept awake by what's on your mind, you might need to work on worrying thoughts (see Chapter 6) but for now reassure yourself and turn your mind to something pleasant. You can also simply notice the thoughts go by like cars on the road or clouds in the sky rather than getting hooked by them.

You might like to start a gratitude journal (see Chapter 7, page 115) to end the day on a positive note, thinking about at least three things you are grateful for from the day. Our minds are like flashlights: what we focus on is what we see. Choosing to focus on something for which we are grateful, no matter how small, helps us to feel more content and peaceful.

When we are relaxed, we are much more likely to drift off into sleep. It is very helpful to develop a regular routine of stretching, progressive muscle relaxation and abdominal breathing. Start with some gentle stretches prior to bed to release tension in your muscles. Then, you may like to do progressive muscle relaxation, tensing and relaxing your muscles from your arms to your feet (see page 50).

Slowing down your breathing and using mindfulness to

detach from your thoughts once you are in bed will also help you to relax and let go of the day.

If you find it hard to get off to sleep, either at first or when you have woken in the night, try focusing on your breath. You could listen to the sound of your breathing, count each out breath until you reach ten and then start from one again, or feel the breath entering your lungs and imagine it filling and nourishing your body. Relax your muscles and think, 'What can I let go?' Or choose a calming word or phrase and repeat it in time with your breathing: 'calm and safe', 'warm and well', or something that has meaning for you, such as a short prayer or mantra.

If you go several nights with very little sleep — maybe only an hour or two — ask your pharmacist or health practitioner for some herbal supplements to help you sleep. You may need to see your doctor for medication. Most doctors will only prescribe enough sleeping pills for a week or so. This is usually enough to get the routine established and then it will be up to you to keep it on track.

4. Eat well

People who are depressed might have no appetite and might not eat enough to maintain their normal weight. Or they might snack on comforting foods and gain weight. Some might have iron or vitamin deficiencies.

A real basic for mood management is a healthy diet. Aim to have three meals a day and look for a balance of carbohydrate (that's bread, rice or starchy vegetables such as potatoes), protein (meat, fish, eggs or nuts) and vegetables. You are probably used to hearing about five+ fruit and vegetable servings per day but researchers are now suggesting this is a minimum and we are healthier if we eat more.

The World Health Organization suggests that the five+ should amount to 400 grams or two and a half to three cups, with a portion being 80 grams or one cup of leafy greens and half a cup of cooked or raw fruit or vegetables. Fruit such as apples and oranges fit well with this definition, a whole fruit being about 80 grams or half a cup. Another way to think of your fruit and vegetable intake could be in at least five handfuls. The main point is that we all need plenty of fruit and vegetables for a healthy diet and they affect not only physical health but mental health and mood.

To make sure you have balance in your diet, include a variety of colours on your plate. If your meal is mainly beige or brown, you might have too many carbs or too much fried food. Green, orange, purple and yellow vegetables contribute different minerals and vitamins to meet your needs. Try to vary what you eat from day to day to cover all the bases. If you snack between meals try to make it something healthy such as fruit, carrot sticks or nuts and keep it small so that you don't spoil your appetite for the meal that's coming up.

If you don't feel hungry you may have to 'eat by numbers' — have the meal because it's what you do at breakfast or lunchtime — and have as balanced a meal as possible. Try to encourage yourself to eat by making the food look attractive and setting yourself a place at the table. If you are eating alone, put on some music or use the radio for company. Depression can reduce self-esteem so that it is hard to believe you are worth a good meal and a place at the table. Doing this for yourself can help you to feel cared about and is a small step towards improving your self-worth.

If you are grazing and overeating, the simple ritual of preparing a meal and eating it at the table may slow down that behaviour and make a proper meal more attractive. You will probably feel more satisfied afterwards and less inclined to snack, but it takes time to re-train the habit. Ask yourself, 'Was that enough? Do I feel full?' and try to wait at least 15 minutes before adding to your meal because it takes a while for the satiety (fullness) signals to kick in. You can reassure yourself that it's okay to feel a little hungry between meals, there will be plenty when the time comes.

If you find yourself at the pantry or fridge looking for a snack, try asking, 'What do I really need?' It might not be food. If your energy is low the solution could be as simple as a drink of water or a nap. If you are comfort eating, is there a non-food way you can settle yourself or give yourself a treat? Maybe someone in your life could connect with you through a conversation or a hug.

While it's not a good idea to think about foods as 'good' or 'bad' — all foods make a contribution to a healthy diet — recent information about sugar advises us to carefully monitor our intake of this because it has a powerful effect on many aspects of wellbeing. One problem with sugar intake is the 'boom and bust' effect it can have on your blood sugar, as the sweet treat gives a boost that is followed by a dip in energy and often in mood. It's easy to get on a rollercoaster with this as you seek that sweet boost every time your energy plummets.

The World Health Organization recommends a maximum of six teaspoons of free sugar — that's sugar that is added to food — per day. Those who add sugar to tea and coffee quickly reach their limit, even without taking into account all the hidden sugar in products such as sauces, spreads and even peanut butter, let alone that cake or muffin that goes so well with a hot drink. Reduce your intake of cakes and confectionery, try to avoid sugary soft drinks (sodas) and use a sweetener in hot drinks or leave sugar out altogether. In time you will be satisfied with finding your everyday sweet treats in fresh or dried fruit, where the sugars are a natural component, and you can keep the more indulgent foods for special occasions.

Eating foods rich in minerals and vitamins can boost energy and mood. Being low in iron can cause a lack of energy and other symptoms that mimic depression. If you think you might have an iron deficiency see your doctor for a blood test; it might be necessary to take iron supplements for a while. There is credible research to show that many people with low mood benefit from taking a professionally selected range of micro-nutrients, but these have been given in doses well above the levels you'd find in over-the-counter vitamin tablets.[4]

Serotonin is an important neurotransmitter that has an effect on mood and is created in the digestive system from tryptophan, an amino acid found in many protein foods including meat, fish, dairy products and eggs, as well as plant proteins such as nuts, seeds, oats and chickpeas. Dates and chocolate also contain tryptophan, so it's not only their sweetness that gives a boost to mood. Be moderate in your consumption of chocolate as a mood booster, though, because of the sugar in it. Omega 3 in fish oil is good for many aspects of mental wellbeing and can improve mood. Try to eat fish more than once a week, or talk to a naturopath or pharmacist about taking fish oil supplements. For vegetarians, flaxseed oil is an equivalent source of omega 3. Vitamin B complex can also be helpful if there has been a lack in your diet.

Overall, sound scientific research has shown that a healthy diet has a strong and lasting positive effect on mood. The 'Mediterranean diet' is often referred to, but a variety of eating patterns can improve mood as long as there is plenty of fresh fruit and vegetables, protein from fish, dairy products, nuts and seeds, and small amounts of meat. Carbohydrates are necessary for energy but need to be consumed in moderate amounts. A vegetarian or vegan diet can be very healthy if care is taken to get a good amount of protein.

When thinking about food, ask yourself, 'How can I take the best care of myself with food?'

5. Exercise

We are born to move. You'll know that if you've ever watched a child trying to sit still or observed a baby lying on the mat. Everything is in motion. If an adult tried to imitate such movements, we'd be exhausted in a few minutes. But for all of us, our muscles love to move and our brains are soothed by the rhythm of any repetitive action: walking, dancing, swimming, sitting and clapping along to music — it's all good for us.

Aerobic exercise — that's any exercise that makes you breathe faster — releases endorphins and creates a positive mood. Because of the loss of motivation and the general slowing down that go with depression, it is easy to give up exercise. Even if you don't feel like it, exercise will be essential in helping yourself out of depression, so again, do it by numbers if you find it hard to find motivation.

A minimum of 30 minutes a day is recommended, so that's a good goal to aim for. If you have been quite inactive, start very gently and work up in small steps. You could see a doctor to check what is best for you, but most people can manage a 10-minute walk around the block or a few stretches in the living room. Even if you do physical work, some gentle exercise is still helpful to relax you and activate the pleasure centres in your brain.

If you are not usually active or are not mobile there are exercises you can do while seated. Recently I joined in a session of seated tai chi at my mother's aged care home and was surprised how much of a workout it was. A quick search online will bring up a variety of programs, some with video instructions to follow.

But if possible, get out in the fresh air. A walk on the beach or in a park has the added benefit of taking you into natural surroundings, combining the enjoyment of nature with your exercise program. As we become increasingly urbanized, researchers are beginning to understand that lack of access to nature increases levels of depression and anxiety.

Dr Gregory Bratman of Stanford University had a group of healthy volunteers go for a walk in the San Francisco Bay area. Half the volunteers walked along a busy street while the rest did a nature walk where they had views of the mountains and the bay. After the walks, those from the nature walk reported lower levels of anxiety, negative feelings and rumination. When blood flow and brain activity were measured it was found that a particular area of the brain, in the prefrontal cortex, was less active. This is the area associated with worry and going over and over a problem. The nature walk had freed the walkers from their worries, not just while on the walk but for a time afterwards. [5]

There are many other research projects that look at our relationship with nature and the wellbeing it can bring. In Japan, 'forest bathing' is a popular concept for reducing stress and its good effects have been well documented there, while in New Zealand 'garden therapy' is being studied.[6] A specially planted garden in the Auckland University of Technology campus has been developed to find out what kinds of natural surroundings are most beneficial for our wellbeing. These studies provide useful information to urban planners about the need to include parks and gardens in cities, and they also help to explain why we seek out holidays by the sea or in the mountains to increase our contact with nature.

Not all of us can go on such holidays, however, and even if we can they tend to be infrequent events. We need smaller, more regular natural experiences. Can you find a garden, a tree to sit under or a park to walk in? Perhaps you can use part of your weekend to go hiking in the hills. Some people arrange to walk with friends, adding a third benefit — social contact. Others find a daily walk is a great opportunity for some precious time alone.

While walking is very simple and in the main costs little or nothing at all, there are as many ways to get exercise as there are ways to move your body. Going to the gym is motivating for many because they like the routine, it can be done in all weathers and there is the example of other people exercising, as well as the opportunity for a personal trainer to help you find what you need to do.

Yoga and tai chi have been shown to help with depression and anxiety, perhaps because they are relaxing as well as strengthening. Pilates improves strength and co-ordination, translating into better posture in day-to-day activities. Dancing is good exercise — anything from salsa to Zumba — and has the bonus of music and company. Formal sessions of these types of exercise will generally happen only once a week, so make sure you get another form of exercise on the other days. This could include dancing or doing your yoga or tai chi at home, of course.

There are so many ways to get exercise and many of them come with added extras such as company, music, team spirit (as in team sports), improved co-ordination, interaction with animals and so on. The main thing is to make it fun and fit it into your life so that you will want to exercise regularly. Work out what's best for you and what will fit into your lifestyle.

Think about your personality and what usually motivates you. For some it will be easier to exercise with someone else or a group because you are happier in the company of others and more likely to turn up when you don't want to let people down. If you are this kind of person you might want to join an exercise class or a walking group, or play a team sport.

Others want results and enjoy seeing progress. Gym work with a personal trainer can work well for you, or setting small goals such as timing yourself for a walk around the block and seeing if you can improve on your time or distance. Keep records or graphs and put them where you can see and enjoy them. You could build in small rewards when you reach certain milestones.

If you are craving peace and harmony, find a way of exercising that can bring this to you: take a solo walk in a place you find tranquil, swim laps with mindful attention on your body in the water but without trying to beat any records. If you have the means, exercise to music that makes you feel content and relaxed. Focusing on your body in motion can be very centring and relaxing.

Exercise can also bring something to your life that is lacking elsewhere. For example, if you find your job mundane, challenge yourself to take part in a competition. Or if you work alone you might really enjoy a team sport on your days off. Use exercise to bring balance to your life.

Don't be put off by age or other limitations. We can all improve, given time, patience and support. I was 58 years old when I began to learn to swim. Some childhood experiences had implanted fear and convinced me I was not a swimmer, but with a sensitive and skilled instructor I have been able to learn to trust my body in water and now I swim 1 kilometre (just over ½ a mile) three times a week. Although it took almost five years to achieve the comfort and distance I wanted, there were huge physical and mental benefits right from the start: I quite quickly became fitter, lost a little weight, overcame back pain that had dogged me for years and made some good friends along the way. I had never been 'sporty', so if I can do it, almost anyone can.

So, up off that couch and get to it. Start small and if you are not sure what you would enjoy, sample a number of different things or try to remember what you used to do in the past. If you are not yet at the stage where you can enjoy anything, set a small goal such as a 10-minute walk, and aim to build up from there. Do it at first because it's good for you and in time you will come to enjoy it and even to look forward to it.

NOW: SCHEDULE IT

When you're depressed, facing the day can feel like facing the void. Set yourself a program because it helps a lot to know what you are going to do when you get up in the morning.

Create a timetable and make sure each of the five basics is on it. Alongside each activity note a number from 1 to 10 (1 being the most down you could be, 10 completely happy) that tells how you were feeling at the time. This will help you to work out which activities are the most effective ones for improving your mood.

Keeping records helps you track progress. When you're feeling negative, it's easy to forget that there have been better days. Check back on your records and see if there is any pattern developing.

Make sure you put some things on your timetable that you know are easy to achieve. If you always get up and have a shower, put that on anyway. It will be rewarding to tick it off and it will help you to move on to the next task. This is not cheating — it's motivating yourself!

Sample timetable

The numbers in each cell indicate how much the event was enjoyed, with 10 being the most enjoyable.

Time	Monday	Tuesday	Wednesday	Thursday	Friday
8 am	Get up, shower	Get up, shower	Get up, shower	Get up, shower x (slept till 10 am)	Get up, shower
	Breakfast 3	Breakfast 3	Breakfast 4	Breakfast x	Breakfast 5
10 am	Walk 6	Walk 6	Walk 7	Walk x	Walk 7
12 pm	Lunch 2	Lunch 3	Lunch 3	Lunch 2	Lunch 4
1 pm	Do relaxation to tape x	Do relaxation to tape 3	Do relaxation to tape x	Do relaxation to tape 3	Do relaxation to tape x
3 pm	Library 6	Visit E 5	Computer time 6	Grocery shopping 2	Visit Mum 7
6 pm	Dinner 4	Dinner 4	Dinner 4	Dinner 4	Dinner 4
	TV 5	TV 5	Read 8	TV 5	TV 5
11 pm	Bedtime	Bedtime	Bedtime x (late)	Bedtime	Bedtime

This is a timetable for someone who is not in work or caring for children and only covers the weekdays. For many people the routine on the weekend differs from weekdays: it might be more relaxed with activities timed less precisely and there could be other family members around to spend time with. For a start, structuring just some of the week is fine. If your working week is already structured, you might like to use the weekend for activities you know will be good for your wellbeing.

By looking at the way the schedule is filled in you can see that this person did not enjoy the relaxation exercise and did not do it every day (marked with an 'x' when not done) even though it was scheduled. There will be another way to relax that is more motivating, perhaps by listening to music instead of doing the muscle-relaxing program. On the other hand, walking became more enjoyable as the week went on, and reading was a very positive thing to do, even though the usual pattern was to watch TV with less enjoyment. Note that not going to bed at the set time on Wednesday night put the next day's schedule out badly, but by getting back on track the enjoyment ratings increased. The lifestyle in this program is a very solitary one and as this routine becomes more established, it would be good to add in more activities that involve contact with people. Eating lunch alone does not look very rewarding with a rating of 4; perhaps sometimes it would be good to have lunch with a friend. It might be possible to meet someone for coffee in the afternoon or invite someone round in the evening — socializing doesn't have to involve expense.

There is a page at the back of this book where you can write your own schedule (see page 170). Once all the basics are in place, aim to keep them up for a few weeks until a routine is established. For many people, this alone is enough to create an improvement. However, many people find it hard to take care of themselves, even when they know that they should. If you find that your timetable is still blank at the end of the week and that even if you made a list you have yet to tick anything off on it, you are going to have to back up and look at your blockers. These are the self-defeating thought patterns that could block you from doing everyday things that could make you feel better. This is the next stage.

HOW THEY GOT ON

Let's check in with our case studies to see how they're going.

Laura

Dave and I talked about what I needed. We agreed to share getting up to Josh and on the weekends we took turns to have a sleep-in. It made a big difference to how I was feeling if I could get a bit more sleep. I had my iron levels checked and the doctor recommended a supplement and advised me to increase my intake of protein while I was breastfeeding. I also made sure that I went for a walk every day. Josh would sleep in the pram, so it was a relaxing time for me as well as good exercise.

Jackson

Dad got rid of most of the booze and he and Mum just had an occasional wine. Then he got me out on bike rides and challenged me to take up running again. I wasn't keen on that but when he offered a gym membership I took him up on it. For a while we went together three times a week, but then Dad got busy. I was keen enough to keep going by myself and when there was a chance of a free assessment I toughened up and booked a session with a trainer. That was nerve-wracking, I nearly didn't go, but he was cool. He said I'd done well so far and he showed me how to improve. It became fun and was something to do after school that was better than being in my room. Mum chipped in too with an eating plan — she's a great cook, so she really wanted to build me up and I wasn't going to say no! We had dinner together most nights and had more to talk about.

Josie

The counsellor gave me some breathing exercises to do when I felt like cutting. I had to lie on my bed and take slow breaths till the feeling passed. It seemed pretty unlikely to me, but I tried it and it did help. She also made me a special relaxation recording, which we worked out together. It described me going to my favourite place and feeling safe and happy. When I was little I used to climb a tree in my Nanna's garden and sit up in the leaves where no one could see me. Since Nanna died and the house has been sold I haven't been able to go to that tree, but it was almost as good imagining it. Mum got very strict about proper meals and bedtimes, which was a bit of a bore but I let her do it because the counsellor said she needed to feel helpful. And it was good not to feel so tired and stressed out. I guess all those things helped.

Tom

The psychologist tried to explain to me how to relax and what to do to get a good night's sleep, but to tell the truth the best cure was getting back to work. I finished the day tired enough to sleep at night and I was too busy to dwell on what might have been wrong with my life. I did take the hint about needing some relaxation, though. I made sure that I sat and watched TV with Sally some evenings and that we went for long walks on the weekend. It helped that I was working for someone else, so knock-off time was five o'clock and that was that. Doing a physical job was good for me; I lost a bit of weight and felt fitter.

Kathy

I've always been a bit obsessive about getting enough sleep and exercise and eating the right things. Maybe that was my way of keeping in control. So I didn't have much to change on that score. What I found most difficult was taking time out for myself to relax or to do something I enjoy. I couldn't just lie still and listen to music but I did start taking an hour in the evening to read before I went to bed. I've always loved reading and never let myself have time for it. It's been great and I sleep much better when I take the time to wind down. It's part of my routine now.

6.

MIND POWER:
WHAT WE THINK,
FEEL AND BELIEVE

Depression has a powerful effect on our mind and emotions. Many people find that their concentration for simple things such as reading the newspaper or following a conversation, let alone doing complex tasks, is quite depleted. Positive emotions such as enjoyment, excitement or even love are greyed out while negative emotions of hopelessness and self-criticism take over.

There is a brain-based reason for this. The path to the over-cautious right prefrontal cortex is being strengthened while the more optimistic left prefrontal cortex is neglected. Neuroscientists like to say that 'neurons that fire together, wire together'.[1] That is, the more we take a certain path in our minds, the stronger and clearer that path becomes and the more likely it is that we will take the path again — like those tracks people wear into the grass when they take a short-cut across a corner of a park.

The good news is that the brain is constantly reshaping its

pathways. We can change how we think, by using strategies that strengthen our positive brain-paths and create more resilient tracks for our minds to go down. [2]

FOCUS

An important aspect of this process is attention. Our attention, as I mentioned in the previous chapter, is like a flashlight that illuminates what it shines on. Most of us take attention for granted as if it were something like digestion over which we have little control. In fact, it is more like a muscle that can be developed with exercise. Psychologists have picked up the term 'mindfulness' from Eastern religions, which use meditation as a central tool, but attention has always been of interest to psychologists, teachers and students of all kinds because it is the basis of learning.

To develop your attention, take short moments throughout the day to notice where your mind is focusing its beam and make a decision about whether this is what you want to light up and for how long. Most of us will find that our mind jumps around, and if we bring it back to the subject we choose to attend to, it will either wander from one idea to the next quite randomly or persistently return to some negative preoccupation. With practice we can gain some control over it, sometimes needing to say 'No!' firmly as you would to a small child or a pet in order to keep our attention out of areas that cause us problems.

Dwelling on negative thoughts and worries is called ruminating, which is what a cow does as it chews and re-chews the grass in its stomachs. Sometimes simply noticing and naming the fact that you are ruminating can help you move on from the thoughts. It might even give you a laugh as you picture the cow with green drool coming out of the corner of its mouth … well, let's not go there!

That last sentence illustrates an important point. It's not easy to eliminate a thought. Try not to think of an elephant. No, really, put it out of your mind. No elephant! Hard, isn't it? To put a thought out of our mind, first we must think of it and then try to dismiss it, so that it ends up in the background, like the ghost in the *Ghostbusters* logo.

Now send your elephant into the forest until it is hidden by trees. What do you see this time? Just the trees?

My point is, if you want to banish negative thoughts you are going to have to replace them with something else, just as you might distract a two-year-old from playing in the rubbish bin by offering an interesting toy. Switch the beam of your flashlight on to something else, because it's very hard (and usually not even desirable) to turn the flashlight off. The brain, like nature, abhors a vacuum.

In Chapter 7 we will look at meditation and mindfulness in more detail, because there are techniques for making your flashlight laser-accurate. For now, be aware of where your attention goes to during the day and continue to bring it back to where you want to focus. Don't get frustrated about this process. Scanning the internal and external landscape is what the mind does, checking on our safety. With practice you can gain more control over your mind's focus and get the result you are looking for, whether that is to be more effective at your work or to feel more at peace.

Ideally, unless you really intend to recall something from the past or remember how to do a task you have not done in a while, your attention will be on the present moment, whether that is the job in hand, your experience of your surroundings or paying attention to the conversation you are having. It sounds quite simple when said like that, but our minds are continually time travelling between the past and the future. This is useful in many ways because we learn skills and develop relationships by building on past experiences and we use these to predict future outcomes and plan ahead. But for many of us this is being overdone to an extent that causes harm. The mind becomes bogged down in fear and regret, making safety in the moment elusive even when there is no harm or danger present. Learning to settle into the present moment can be very relaxing and enjoyable.

SELF-TALK

More than most, depressed people can find themselves highlighting and remembering one negative event and overlooking any number of positives, but we all have a bias towards the negative as our brain seeks to make us safe from danger or social embarrassment. To maintain a positive mood it is important to monitor your self-talk and build up your ratio of positive thoughts.

You can test any negative thoughts by reviewing all the information and recognizing the times when you are generalizing or anticipating the worst-case scenario. Ask: what's the evidence for this? What standard am I using to make this judgment? Notice how easy it is to perceive failure when you make comparisons with a mythical ideal rather than a realistic standard.

For example, when Tom took the job in a plant nursery, he could have made himself even more depressed by thinking that the job was beneath him and regretting the loss of his business.

However, he wisely compared his feelings about going to work with how miserable he would be if he just sat on the couch. Using that as his measure, he was able to find satisfaction in the new work and even appreciate how pleasant it was not to have much responsibility.

It may also be hard to see anything positive in the future. Monitor your thinking and pick up on any running commentary that is just running you down. Take a neutral stance and wait to see how things turn out — it's much more relaxing than always expecting the worst. As folk wisdom has it, 'Cross the bridge when you come to it'. When you think about that saying you can see that there is really no other way. Unless thinking ahead is contributing something useful to your planning and preparation, such as studying for an exam, worrying only uses your imagination to torture yourself. Why do that?

Do your best to prepare for whatever you are aiming for, then let go of your attachment to the outcome. If you've done your best, whatever happens, happens. It's as if you have planted something; say, a lavender bush. You can't guarantee how it will turn out but you can give it the conditions it needs — soil, water, sunlight — and then let it flourish as well as it can. It helps, too, if you expect it just to be a lavender bush and not to give you roses or apples!

Ask yourself: What would my life be like if I thought less and focused more on the task at hand?

So, take some time to examine your thoughts and notice how they might affect your mood.

On the next page is an example of someone working through their feelings about committing to an exercise timetable and attempting to change their thinking from vulnerable to more helpful, resilient thinking.

Problem	Vulnerable thinking	Resilient thinking
Writing a timetable	I can't get motivated to sort this out.	I can create a routine, it will help me.
Mental chit-chat (the thoughts that block you or help you)	I'm too tired. It won't work anyway. I can't get up that early. I hate exercise.	It might be worth a try. I used to get up for work okay. It can't be any worse than I feel now.
Beliefs (What are the underlying beliefs and emotions?)	I don't have any willpower. I'm really sick. It's not fair to make me. It's too simple to work.	I can just do it. I can overcome depression. No one is forcing me but I do want to feel better.
Consequences (What will happen if I follow my thoughts?)	I'll stay the same and feel ashamed I didn't try. I'll keep worrying that I'm ill. My life will be empty. My family will feel let down.	I will feel proud of myself for making the effort. I might get fitter and feel better. I might be able to enjoy some things. My family and friends will feel proud of me for trying.

Choose a problem and make a table to clarify your thoughts, using the blank table at the back of this book or by creating one of your own (see page 169). Change your vulnerable thinking into resilient thinking. Remember, hope is an important human value and staying optimistic is a discipline, something to be cultivated.

TEN QUESTIONS TO CHALLENGE YOUR NEGATIVE THOUGHTS

1. What is the thought?
2. Do I believe it?
3. What is the evidence for this thought?
4. What is the evidence against it?
5. Is it permanent or will it pass with time?
6. What will happen if this thought is true?
7. Could I live with the consequences?
8. Can I do something about it? If so, what?
9. What would happen if I don't believe this thought?
10. What would I tell a good friend who had this thought?

Write out your answers to these questions. Read through them, adapting them until you feel calm and can let go of the thought.

SELF-BULLYING

Many people have a voice in their head that evaluates everything they do and makes comments, often very cruel ones, about them. Think about what you are saying to yourself. Would you say such things to your best friend?

Sometimes that critical voice comes from childhood, maybe from comments by a parent as you were growing up or from being bullied by peers at school. You might have taken on the job of scolding yourself in an effort to 'get up to scratch' and in the hope that eventually your parent would love you and praise you or you would make friends. Some people feel they have to nag themselves to get motivated, and the apathy of depression makes that seem even more true.

But it's well proven that we do all better with a carrot than a stick. In so many areas — child-rearing, education, business — it is understood that people need praise and encouragement and will thrive in a positive atmosphere in which they get feedback that they are doing well and are appreciated.

Think about a child learning to walk. Each skill the child practises is greeted with praise and excitement from the parents: pulling herself up to stand with the support of furniture, standing alone, walking with support, taking the first step. The child herself shows pleasure in each achievement and practises over and over. We don't criticize the child for sitting down heavily when she loses her balance, or tell her she's not learning as fast as other children. Not at all; we share her joy in each little achievement and encourage her to keep practising.

If you can be as encouraging as that to yourself in whatever you want to achieve, you can make progress and feel good about yourself.

WHAT DO YOU SAY ABOUT YOURSELF?

Write down some of the negative comments you make to yourself. It might take a while to catch exactly what is going through your mind because the thoughts are often automatic. Write them down as you notice them. When you have as many as you can catch, have a look at them on the page. Would you really expect someone to feel good about themselves and be able to achieve much with all that going on?

Now take a new sheet of paper and write down some positive thoughts to put in their place. Many people find this very difficult. The thought comes back: 'Well I really have failed!' and replacing it with 'I am not a failure' is like trying not to think of an elephant. You don't want to lie to yourself but find something realistic you can agree with, for example:

- 'I'm doing my best and when I know better I'll do better.'
- 'Doing this exercise is a start.'
- 'I made a mistake but it's in the past now.'

The aim is to replace the critical, nagging voice with an encouraging, coping voice. Be aware that self-criticism separates us from others by focusing on how we are different: 'You should be able to do that. Everyone else can!' Being kind to ourselves (see 'Compassion' on page 116 in Chapter 7) links us to others by finding the common ground: 'You're feeling tired and discouraged. Poor you! Anyone would feel like that after such a week!' Once you fully acknowledge how you feel and accept that it is part of being human to feel bad at times, you may be surprised how much easier it is to recover and turn your mind to more positive things.

IT'S NOT ALL YOUR FAULT

Depression comes with feelings of guilt and low self-esteem, which can make it very hard to evaluate a situation objectively.

'Is the boss at work bullying me or am I doing a really poor job?'

'Should I leave this relationship or would my partner be more loving if only I wasn't depressed?'

Questions like these can be very hard to sort out in the midst of depression. This isn't the best time to make major decisions. After all, difficulty making decisions is one of the symptoms of depression (remember that reduced blood flow to the frontal lobes?).

However, in some instances it really is the situation that causes the depression. If you suspect that is so, try to talk it over with someone who can give you objective feedback. It may take a while to come to any conclusion, but there are definitely times when you can benefit from leaving a toxic situation.

It may be that the situation is not in itself toxic but is not a good fit for you. For example, an introvert might find a very busy, people-focused sales job too draining to be sustainable, or a creative person might struggle in a data-entry situation that would suit someone who likes clear rules and instructions. Becoming aware of the lack of fit can give you an opportunity to talk with your manager about adapting the work in some way, or you may be able to use your skills and talents in your time outside work. For example, the data entry operator might have a vibrant other life in amateur theatre. But if it is clear that your circumstances are contributing to your depression, look at how you could make changes.

If you are being hurt physically or emotionally, seek help to find safety. It will be very hard to overcome depression while you are at risk of actual harm.

FEELINGS

The words 'feelings' and 'emotions' are often used interchangeably, as I do in this book because it seems more natural. Strictly speaking, feelings arise when your brain detects information from the environment through your eleven senses (did you think there were only five?):

Sight

Hearing

Taste

Smell

Heat

Cool

Pain

Pleasure

Balance (vestibular system)

Pressure

Motion (kinaesthetic)

These senses help you to find out what is going on in the world by feeding data into your nervous system.

Emotions, on the other hand, are what those feelings mean. They are short-lived and subjective, shaped by experiences and perceptions. There are several different theories about what the basic emotions are and where they are sited in the brain. Therapists and researchers working with the emotions come up with different lists and some cultures have words for emotions that don't translate easily into other languages. Broadly speaking, we can generally agree on six: happiness, fear, anger, disgust, surprise and sadness, but there are many finer details within these. For example, happiness could include pride, joy, success, love, ecstasy, contentment, fondness, and so on. The bigger our vocabulary for emotions, the more we can both understand others and clarify to ourselves what we feel.

There are myths about emotions, such as that they are hard-wired and cannot change. Simply not true! Our emotions are interpretations of our experiences and often change hugely depending on changes in our knowledge and understanding. That is why the saying 'to understand is to forgive' is relevant: with better knowledge, anger might change to compassion.

Another myth is that it is childish to show how we feel, or that women are more emotional than men. Many people undervalue and seek to deny their emotions. In my work and in my own life I have found that emotions provide valuable information and guidance. You could even say that emotion is the primary motivational system and I have often seen that this is the case. Accepting and expressing emotion appropriately is a skill of growing up. That doesn't mean uncontrolled venting, of course, but denying or burying emotion is not helpful.

Work by Paul Gilbert identifies three systems that underlie our feelings and actions.[3] They are:

- threat and self-protection
- incentive and resource-seeking
- soothing and contentment.

Each has a vital part to play in life, but if these three systems get out of balance or become patterned in certain ways, we can suffer.[4]

Let's look at them one at a time.

Threat and self-protection

This system, otherwise known as fight-or-flight, is one we have in common with most living beings. It creates feelings of anger or fear in order to protect us.

In the natural world it is vital to work out whether that rustle in the bushes means that you are about to find your own dinner or be someone else's dinner, and to react quickly. It works on a 'better safe than sorry' theory, so the alarm is triggered almost instantly, creating a feeling of dread and a strong desire to escape or a rush of aggression to prepare to fight for survival.

Anger

When we get angry the 'fight' part of the system is kicking in to deal with the threat by going on the offensive. The anger tells us when someone is invading our space or infringing our rights. It lets us know that something needs to be dealt with and it provides the energy and motivation to do the job. Anger often comes from disappointment due to the gap between what was expected and what actually happened.

Angry people pull themselves up to their full height and make big gestures to increase their size and look intimidating (think of an angry cat with its fur bristling right down to its tail). Going red in the face, glaring and using a loud tone of voice add to the effect. If you are faced with an angry person you need to avoid matching anger with anger, which will escalate the conflict. It is better to speak softly, give the person plenty of space and if possible leave the situation, returning to talk about the matter when you are both calmer. When the brain is in fight-or-flight mode, it is much harder to think clearly, because emotional information from the limbic system, the centre in the mid-brain that receives and manages emotion, dominates the more rational messages of the cortex.

If it's you who is getting angry, take time out and regulate your breathing (see pages 44–49 for breathing exercises) until you feel a slower, rhythmic breath return. When you have had time to recover and think things through, see if you can go back and calmly sort the matter out. Bottling things up is not a good option but neither is the 'let it all out' approach, which might give relief in the short term but it is rarely effective in getting your needs met and could damage relationships, sometimes irretrievably. When someone has a tantrum, what they said and what it was really about usually gets lost in the emotional storm, and all that anyone will remember is the tantrum. We generally try to avoid angry people. This is not useful for bringing about change and improving relationships. Also, depressed people are prone to guilt and shame, so they may well feel worse after blowing their top than they did before.

If you feel yourself succumbing to anger, do something physical, such as going for a brisk walk or digging in the garden, or cleaning something if you need to stay inside. Your muscles will want to be active to disperse physical changes made by the angry feelings. Anger is energy and like any other energy it can be put to use through exercise, work or creativity. You may find that not only does the exercise disperse the emotional tension, the fresh air and sense of achievement restore your equilibrium. Once you have got over your anger, you can carry on with the task and enjoy yourself. In that more resilient emotional state you will be better equipped to decide whether to let go of the matter that offended you or to return and sort it out through discussion.

Notice that I am not recommending dispersing anger through venting. Shouting, punching a pillow or throwing things, even in private, all tend to increase angry feelings rather than reduce them.

Fear

The 'flight' part of the system is the choice to leave the scene and avoid the threat. This reaction creates feelings of hyper-alertness, physical tension, shortness of breath and a sense of fear, due to the effects of hormones preparing the body for action. People who have been traumatized can stay hyper-vigilant for long periods of time, and are easily triggered by reminders of the trauma. An example is the returned soldier who is afraid of thunder or the sudden sound of a car backfiring because it triggers the fear of gunfire. We can all be 'gun-shy' about things that frightened or harmed us in the past, because we are primed to seek safety.

Avoiding our fears can make life very narrow, because the brain's ability to make rapid associations links one thing after another with the original fear, creating a long chain of things to avoid. For example, a person who had a panic attack in the supermarket due to being tired, hungry and stressed when tackling the shopping might avoid that particular supermarket, then all supermarkets, then all shops, then streets with shops on them ... you see where this is going. Fear can make you a prisoner in your own home.

When talking about fear I like to think of the way a herd of horses, when startled, will instinctively gallop to the end of the paddock but then turn and face whatever set them off. From a safe distance, fears can be approached one step at a time. We have the ability to rethink and assess situations so we can face our fears. Often they turn out to be not so terrifying after all.

Small steps allow us to face our fears while staying calm. This is called desensitization and is often used by psychologists to treat fears and phobias.

Freeze

There is a third aspect to the safety system: 'freeze'. It's what small animals do in response to a threat they cannot outrun or fight off. To freeze means to stay very still, breathe very lightly and hope not to be noticed. People who have had a traumatic childhood often use this option, holding back from giving their point of view, aiming to stay under the radar. Their breathing may be affected and they might need to retrain this due to a tendency to hold the breath when stressed. A long-standing freeze response will contribute significantly to depression. Good breathing and a strong, open posture can be powerful antidotes.

Is it really a threat?

In adult life, most of us rarely have to deal with the kind of threat you fight or run away from. Many of our fears are worries about things that have not yet happened and may never happen. Ruminating on worst-case scenarios creates strongly unpleasant feelings as the brain and body prepare to struggle for survival. The fight-or-flight response does not discriminate between imagination and reality, nor does it necessarily detect the difference between a small threat and a serious one, so self-protection might come out fighting in response to a minor provocation or it might fearfully avoid a situation that actually is not at all dangerous.

You might find yourself asking 'What if ...' very often. This is an attempt to use our imagination to prepare for future problems and the key thing is that at this stage they are imaginary. We can prepare — such as keeping a flashlight handy in case of a blackout — but we can't prevent the problem. Do your preparation and then let go, trusting that if a crisis occurs you will be resourceful at the time.

Incentive and resource-seeking

This drive gives us the motivation to meet our needs. The pleasure of meeting a goal can range from the buzz of racing a friend to the end of the swimming pool to the excitement of romantic love. Used positively, this system can be energizing and stimulating, but it can also cause frustration if our goals are thwarted or take longer to achieve than we expect.

Some people throw everything they have at this system, never questioning whether their goals are worth all their energy. Many societies admire goal-oriented people who are driven to achieve and who acquire symbols of material wealth such as big houses and flashy cars. Alongside these external rewards, there is an internal reward from the brain's releases of dopamine, the same brain chemical that responds to recreational drugs. And just as those drugs are addictive, we can also get hooked on status, work, money or excitement. Like the drug addict, the high achiever might start to feel caught up, chasing an elusive sense of satisfaction because nothing is ever enough.

Where our basic desire to want 'more and better' was once an asset when it came to finding safer caves and better territory to support the family, now, unchecked, it can cause serious problems. These may take the form of addictions or health problems such as obesity or stress from overwork. Relationships may suffer because of 'keeping your eyes on the prize' and failing to pay attention to family and friends. On a global scale, the overuse of resources threatens the delicate balance of the planet.

Linking this drive with the third system, soothing and contentment, helps to keep it in balance. If it dominates, or worse, links to the threat system so that you become driven by fear or resentment, the need to achieve can become exhausting and destructive to yourself and your relationships.

When in balance, incentive and resource-seeking can provide excitement, challenge and motivation. It can be a source of creativity and good work in the world. It is this drive that people seek to harness when they tell you to 'follow your passion'. But it must be kept in balance.

Soothing and contentment

This emotional regulation system creates a sense of safety and calm. It develops in the bond between the infant and their early caregivers and is continued in adult life through compassion and kindness for ourselves and others. It settles the other two systems and allows us to rest and be at peace in the moment. Throughout life we are attuned to the signals that show us that others care about us: their tone of voice, facial expression, the way they share positive feelings and show an interest in us. Humans are social beings and it is in our nature to notice and respond to others.

It sounds so appealing: who would not want to be in a state of soothing and contentment? Yet many of us spend very little time here. Our 'new mind' skills of thinking and predicting can get caught up in the 'old brain' threat system and cause us to go round in circles with emotions of fear, anger and distress competing for our attention.

The origin of the soothing and contentment system is in the way a parent touches, feeds and comforts their child. Hormones such as oxytocin are released in the brains of both parent and child, bringing a sense of wellbeing and relaxation. Hugs with the people we love recreate this feeling, as can a massage, a warm bath, sunbathing or a relaxing swim.

It is this state that makes compassion and kindness possible. Most of us instinctively know how to care for things, from possessions such as a pot plant or our car, through to our friends or a vulnerable baby. We also care for ourselves to a greater or lesser degree. Learning how to access the soothing and contentment system will help to master depression and feel good.

MANAGE YOUR EMOTIONS

Understanding and managing your emotions are powerful skills for life. To some extent we have all done this in the process of growing up. As babies we cried and stressed about any discomfort, to alert our carers to our needs. As toddlers we threw tantrums when frustrated. We learnt from the reactions of those around us, and from our own responses, how to cope with discomfort and frustration and ideally how to ask for our needs to be met or find ways to meet them ourselves. As our brains develop, the prefrontal cortex grows into its role of evaluating and responding to our inner and outer worlds, integrating our experiences. Emotional regulation is a necessary skill for life and also a lifelong process, because there are always new experiences to integrate.

Here are some tips to make managing strong emotions easier.

1. Put words to your feelings

Identify ways of expressing what you are feeling. At first to yourself: 'I'm getting anxious', 'It's really frustrating being stuck in traffic when I have a meeting to go to', 'I love her'. Then to others about yourself: 'I'm feeling ashamed that I didn't do what I said I would', 'I love you'.

Develop a wide vocabulary of words for emotions and learn to understand how you feel in finer detail. A painter who only knows red, blue and yellow will create much less subtle work than someone who sees the differences in colours such as crimson, cerise, scarlet, brick, turquoise, cobalt, aqua, topaz, citrine and so on. If you have ever owned a big box of crayons you will know there are many more! So it is with emotions.

Are there some emotions you're better at identifying in yourself than others? Many people find it hard to identify when they feel ashamed, for example, but easier to know when they feel anxious.

Can you separate similar emotions? For example, do you know the difference between jealousy and envy? This is a tricky one. Envy occurs when we lack something we see in another person. Jealousy occurs when something we already possess (usually a special relationship) is threatened by a third person. Sometimes both occur together, for example if you fear losing your partner to someone whose power and confidence you envy.

As you become more skilled at naming your feelings you will find that you can make more conscious choices about what to do with them. Even the labelling itself might reduce the intensity as you bring your powerful new brain, the cortex, into the mix, rather than operating solely from your old brain.

It is also important to be able to identify what someone else is feeling. Can you tell when your partner is feeling angry and scared rather than only seeing the anger? Is your co-worker's abrupt tone of voice due to embarrassment? Using more specific labels instead of just saying 'He's in a bad mood' will deepen the information you get in any situation and make it much more useful.

If it seems wise and safe, can you tell the other person what you perceive them to be feeling and ask them to help you understand more fully? Even without voicing it, your more nuanced perception will improve your reaction and ability to communicate.

2. Tolerate your emotions

Until we become comfortable enough with our emotions to name and understand them, we will probably tend to avoid certain emotions by side-stepping situations we know will trigger them.

Can you persist with appropriate goals even if you are feeling anxious? If so, you'll be less likely to avoid trying new things, more likely to try things a second time if it didn't go well the first time and less likely to abandon projects before they've become successful. Persistence is a hallmark of successful people who generally don't give up in the face of a few failures.

In some situations, avoiding uncomfortable feelings can lead to giving up your rights. It is good to learn to communicate clearly even when you feel awkward, such as refusing to buy in the face of a strong sales pitch or telling a friend that you appreciate their support but would prefer to do something your own way.

As you learn to understand your emotions and become comfortable with how you feel, you will be able to have conversations at a more intimate level, bringing in emotional language to communicate in depth. This is important for developing and maintaining friendships and close partnerships.

Avoiding and suppressing strong feelings can create a sense

of loneliness, even when you are with other people, as well as losing the important information such feelings bring. Tolerating negative feelings makes it possible to experience the whole range of emotion with all the colour and energy this brings to your life.

3. Soothe and calm emotions

Develop a range of options for helping yourself feel better when something goes wrong. This is different from denial or suppression of emotions because it starts with naming and acknowledging them, then moves to making choices about how to calm any distress.

You could look at the suggestions from page 44 in Chapter 5 for breathing, relaxation or exercise to calm the physical responses of your emotions. You could develop some kind and supportive sayings to remind yourself that you are a good person doing your best and that bad times pass. You could 'change the channel' by distracting yourself with an activity that will fill your attention and divert your thoughts. Can you check any tendency to judge yourself harshly or bully yourself with 'shoulds'?

Can you comfort other people when they are upset? Many people find this easier than comforting themselves, but some will find that distressing emotions in someone close to them triggers their own distress and makes them want to get away. Can you tolerate this discomfort so that you can help someone else?

In the next chapter we will look at compassion and gratitude and their role in this.

4. Be patient

In the much publicized 'marshmallow experiment' of the 1960s and 70s children were offered a choice between one small reward provided immediately or two small rewards if they waited without eating the treat for a short period, approximately 15 minutes.[5] Follow-up in later years showed that children who could wait achieved better school results and were healthier and more successful in adult life. This experiment has been repeated in recent times with similar results.

Being able to wait for the pay-off is an important skill for success, and the trick is to manage our feelings while waiting. The successful children used all sorts of strategies: hiding their eyes or turning away from the tempting sight of the sweet, singing to themselves, self-talk about waiting for the double treat, all of which we could benefit from as adults. Often, anxiety drives impatience with a feeling of 'Let's get it over with', but simple techniques can calm that anxiety and reassure us that it's okay to wait.

For example, are you able to wait till tomorrow to eat the rest of that dessert when you've already had one portion? (Easier if there are no teenagers in the house to beat you to it!) Can you sit down to your study instead of going out with friends, knowing that in time you will have a feeling of success from your achievement and maybe a better future if you gain a qualification?

Can you say to yourself, about a bad day or a bad feeling, 'This too will pass' and calmly wait it out?

5. Cultivate positive emotions

In an interview, well-known Australian writer Tim Winton said that human beings are 'hard-wired for hope' and 'optimism is a discipline'.[6] These two ideas give a strong basis to the concepts of positive psychology and life coaching, which show us how to live well using habits that probably come naturally to certain positive, successful people but need conscious attention when depression has taken hold.

For example, do you regularly schedule activities you know you'll look forward to? Even small events — a walk in the sun when you take a break from your work, watching a favourite TV program in the evening, putting on some music while you do a chore — can lighten your day. Plans for the weekend, a change of scene or an annual holiday can be savoured as they develop, and the enjoyable activities can punctuate your routine in a positive way.

Here are some tips for creating positive emotions:

- Be realistic and objective about comparing yourself with others. There will always be somebody better than you at some things, and others who lack some of your skills. How you live your own life matters more than what others are doing.
- Avoid killjoy thinking, which drives us to look for the flaws in any success or to look ahead for the next bad thing that could happen, rather than savouring the moment.
- Count your blessings and be grateful for what each day brings.
- Give yourself credit for even small successes and take time to enjoy your feeling of achievement.
- Celebrate and share positive times by telling family and friends. Make an occasion of it by inviting people around for a meal to celebrate with you, or by taking morning tea in to the office to share with your colleagues.

- Be aware of the moment and pay attention to your senses and feelings so that you create lasting memories of what could otherwise be a fleeting experience on the way to the next chore or challenge.
- Think of as many names for positive emotions as you can and list them: joy, courage, excitement, anticipation, surprise and so on. You may experience more of these in a day than you realize.

BELIEFS

Human infants are born at a very early stage of development. Unlike a newborn foal or calf they are unfinished, helpless in many ways but supremely able to adapt to the family and culture into which they arrive. This is an important part of childhood and adolescence as the young person develops into an adult who understands and can function in their environment. The developing brain is geared to learn rapidly and make sense of the world and along the way the child forms beliefs about the nature of things.

Some of those beliefs are formed through direct experience and may not be entirely true but are still perfectly functional. For example, it's natural to believe that the chair on which you sit is a solid object that will hold you securely. That works fine day to day, but in fact, science can tell us that each atom of the chair has more space than substance. So in this case our belief is functional — it's safe to sit down! — but the chair is not really as solid as it seems.

Other beliefs are formed in our relationships and can vary widely depending on how well we have been cared for. Take the common experience of a child who falls and hurts herself. If the parent's response is warm and caring, but matter of fact —

'Where does it hurt? Let me give it a rub. Okay now? Let's go, then.' — the child can learn to cope with small hurts and trust that the adult will know if it is serious. If the parent is harsh about the experience — 'Don't be so clumsy! Stop making a fuss! We'll be late!' — the child may either need to make more of a fuss than is warranted to get her needs met, or may decide that it's useless to expect anyone to care.

This is one common example out of thousands of experiences that shape each one of us as we grow up. Then there are cultural norms and beliefs about food, behaviour, courtesy to others and so on that we learn as children and perceive as the right way to do things. Childhood is a time of rapidly creating a working model of the world and our community. Our beliefs give us a handle on a complex environment.

It can be just as surprising to learn that our take on the world is largely made up of beliefs that vary from person to person and from culture to culture as it is to learn that solid objects are largely made of space. Our world view often feels unchangeable. Questioning it can be a bit disorienting.

Sometimes I ask clients to explore where they think some of their beliefs came from, and often we find that they were formed when the client was quite young. I then ask, 'Is it wise to keep basing your life on what a child thought should happen? Would you like to review some of those beliefs?' Understanding that beliefs are not facts and can be altered and adapted in the light of new information can be very freeing for some people.

I am not talking about spiritual beliefs here (there will be more about this in the next chapter). For now, I am asking you to examine your assumptions about yourself in the world and those around you. These assumptions lead to certain expectations and it is always good to be open to looking at our expectations because unmet expectations can cause anger and disappointment.

You probably feel you have a right to your expectations; for example, that a friend will be punctual if you arrange to meet. Perhaps that's an expectation you have of yourself and you are extending it to other people. But if your friend is consistently late you might have to question whether you are being realistic. Rather than feeling annoyed, you could come a little later yourself, or use the time to catch up on some reading. Or you could explain your expectations to your friend and see if you can find some common ground. For anyone who at this point is saying, 'No! It's right to be punctual!' I'd challenge you to look at this as a belief (or value, see Chapter 7) you hold that others might not share. Can you imagine something else a person might prioritize above punctuality? Giving a friend her full attention or completing a job thoroughly before she leaves for your appointment, perhaps?

Albert Ellis, writing in the 1960s through till his death in 2007 at the age of 93, wrote extensively about the irrational beliefs that cause a lot of human suffering:[7]

- **'This shouldn't be happening!'** So often we are shocked that things don't turn out the way we expect and react with anger or disappointment. If challenged most people would agree that the world is not always fair and we don't always get what we want, but deep down we expect it to be fair to us. If you flick the light switch and the light doesn't come on, you might be annoyed or alarmed that the power is off. But if someone tells you they are just about to change the lightbulb, you understand the situation and feel relieved. Nothing is different — the light still didn't come on — except what you thought and felt about the situation.

- **'I must be perfect.'** It's not possible. And trying to be perfect is bad for your health. You can control your own effort, but not the outcome. 'I will do my best' is rational. 'I must be the best' is not. Sadly, so many people who generously say 'Nobody's perfect' to forgive a friend's mistake, expect themselves to be the exception. Treat yourself like a good friend and accept that you're not perfect. Forgive your own mistakes (see 'Compassion' on page 116 in Chapter 7).
- **'I have to worry about this.'** Worry can seem very compelling, almost as if the mental effort of worrying could work some magic to solve the problem. Not worrying can even cause feelings of anxiety in itself. But a belief that worrying is necessary is not rational. Set a time to worry by saying 'I'll think about that when I get home, but only for half an hour' and at other times, say a firm 'no' to the thoughts. This lets your brain know it doesn't need to keep reminding you. Try to distinguish between worry that goes round and round in circles without getting results, from more rational problem-solving. A repeated worry that can't be problem-solved is a rumination. Bin it!
- **'It's because of my past.'** There are past traumas that cause deep distress and these need to be dealt with in therapy (see Chapter 9). But believing that all your problems are due to your past is very disempowering because we can't change the past. Accept that your past had its challenges, even that you have learnt some bad habits, then set about problem-solving in a more engaged and confident way. If you can, get a friend to help you challenge the unhelpful beliefs.

'Should' and 'shouldn't' are words that let us know we are talking about our beliefs, and that our beliefs are not, at this point, a good fit with reality. Albert Ellis condemned the words 'should' and 'must'. He felt they were at the core of so much of our emotional suffering because they imply that the universe needs to do what we want, which leads to useless protest when things don't go our way. There are many things that are beyond our control. We can 'prefer' them to go our way, but saying 'should' and 'must' is like having a tantrum when we don't like the weather. You think it 'should' be sunny? Well, if it's not, you can't make it so.

When you align your expectations with reality, you can stay calm and think more clearly. This gives you a better chance of working out how to get what you prefer.

Whenever you hear yourself saying 'should' or 'must', it's a sign you could be letting an unhelpful belief take over. It's like using an outdated operating system on the computer. Time to upgrade and get in touch with reality. Can you challenge the unhelpful belief and replace it with something more effective?

To sum up: thoughts, feelings and beliefs guide and shape behaviour, which in turn feeds back into thoughts and feelings and into shaping our beliefs. Being self-aware in these important respects gives us the opportunity to make informed choices for our own wellbeing and that of others in our life. Beliefs can be changed in the light of new information throughout life. Thoughts and feelings do not have to dictate how you live your life; they can be examined and managed. You can h*ave* a feeling or a thought instead of *being* it. Recognize those thoughts and feelings and separate yourself from the various parts of the experience, knowing that they are fleeting aspects of who you really are.

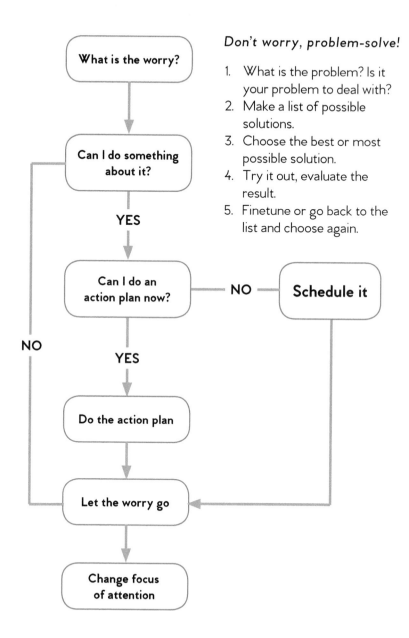

What is the worry?

Can I do something about it?

YES

Can I do an action plan now? — **NO** — **Schedule it**

NO

YES

Do the action plan

Let the worry go

Change focus of attention

Don't worry, problem-solve!

1. What is the problem? Is it your problem to deal with?
2. Make a list of possible solutions.
3. Choose the best or most possible solution.
4. Try it out, evaluate the result.
5. Finetune or go back to the list and choose again.

USE YOUR TALENTS

One more comment about 'mind'. In the course of my work with clients I have seen time and again that under-stimulated minds can do a lot of worrying and ruminating. Take the example of a mother of young children who has given up a challenging job to care for them, or someone who did not get the education their mind was suited to and so has been under-employed in mundane work. Unless such people are resourceful in finding a source of stimulation and mental challenge, it is quite common to find elements of anxiety and depression creating stress as their minds spin their wheels.

We all have gifts and talents, and our special interests are often based on them. Not everyone can find a job that uses their best skills but if not, try to find a way to develop your interests in your spare time. For example, an engineer might do creative woodwork in his garage on the weekends, a teacher may be a keen gardener, the checkout operator may be writing a novel in the evenings. It doesn't have to take the world by storm. Use your gifts because they are yours and you can enjoy them. Others might enjoy the results but that's not the main purpose. Express yourself because you're the only version of you!

HOW THEY GOT ON

Let's take another look at the five people we've been following.

Laura

With the depression I had fallen back into all the old negative thought patterns. I had to be the perfect mother with the perfectly clean and tidy house and I beat myself up for being anything less. The impossibility of it overwhelmed me and that's why I took to my bed. But once I started meeting with the other mothers from the postnatal depression support group I realized how unrealistic I had been. I knew I had mastered that old perfectionism before and I could again. They encouraged me to talk more openly with Dave about how I was feeling. I was so ashamed of being depressed that I had been shutting him out — but of course he could understand and wanted to help. Together we got things back into perspective and established a routine that worked. Dave looked up depression on the internet and it helped to see it as a problem that lots of people have, not something that was my fault or some kind of moral weakness. It didn't go away all at once but by working on it I could feel more in control.

Jackson

When Mum decided to go in for a women's triathlon I found I could help her a bit with her training. Dad said we should watch her on the day but my hands got sweaty thinking about being in the crowd. I went online and found this site that talked about anxiety, so I began doing a daily breathing exercise that was okay. It said to let your thoughts go by like cars on a motorway and I could do that, watching my worries drive away. It felt quite cool. I was really proud when I could go and watch Mum and cheer her on, and Dad and I were proud of her, too.

Josie

I don't usually like being wrong but it was a relief to realize that I was wrong about Mum and Dad not liking me any more. Just because they had split up didn't mean they regretted having me, and once we talked about that it was much better. Of course, they hadn't helped by not having much time for me but when I said what I wanted, they did try. The counsellor explained how cutting was a kind of message, but it's better to say it in words. I do get that now.

Tom

There was quite a lot to sort out in my head. I definitely had to challenge the feeling that I was useless if I wasn't working all the time. I also had to understand that all the doubts about my life were a part of depression and when I looked at things more realistically I could feel proud of my achievements. It was hard talking to Sally more openly, we'd got used to leading our own lives, but I think she was quite happy to hear that I wanted to spend more time with her. She said she'd rather know what was on my mind than just see me looking withdrawn and miserable, so I put it all out there. She took it surprisingly well, even the bit about wondering if life could have been different. She said everyone wonders that. Do they?

Kathy

The therapist tried to help me to be less hard on myself and not to feel everything was my fault. I understood what she meant but it wasn't until the medication kicked in that I could actually feel I was okay. It was like the light switching on. Then we could talk about my family without me feeling so hurt and guilty. I could accept that they hadn't meant me any harm, they just didn't know how to take me. I even handled a situation at work by being more assertive and it worked because I know I looked as if I meant it. I always thought everyone was so much stronger than me because life was so hard and they could handle it where I couldn't. Now I realize that when you're depressed it's like trying to run a race with rocks tied to your feet. Without those rocks, it's not so hard.

7.

SPIRIT: WHAT CONNECTS US?

When I talk about 'spirit' I'm referring to that aspect of ourselves and others that is more than physical. Some call it soul or our higher self, or simply self. It's the part of all of us that seeks meaning and purpose and that connects with other people and the natural world. It is also the connection we have with our true or deeper self.

You may have a spiritual path that nurtures you, perhaps through a particular religion. This has the advantage of offering a structure and some guidelines for how to live a good life and often involves meeting regularly with a group of like-minded people who meditate or worship together. Perhaps in prayer or when hearing an inspiring preacher you feel a deep sense of connection and peace. During your times of worship you might find moments of insight that sustain you and show you your true nature or the direction you need to take in life.

You may find a church or religious group is not for you. That doesn't have to stop you from developing your spiritual nature as you seek to find meaning, connection and the best way to live your life. Perhaps your moments of spiritual peace and insight come when you are listening to music, absorbed in an activity such as a really centred swim or run, or maybe sitting quietly on a beach or in a garden. Notice and treasure such moments.

A common thread for experiencing spiritual deepening is being still, slowing down and being in the present moment. When we are caught up in the inwardness of depression, with a lot of negative mental chatter going on, we can lose sight of our guiding lights and the connections that give life meaning; therefore it becomes even more important to make a conscious effort to nurture our spiritual life.

VALUES

Values are the guiding principles developed as we go through life that underlie the way we live and work. They help us choose our priorities and can show whether life is going the way we want it to. Someone whose behaviour matches their values can be recognized as a person of integrity and will probably feel that life is good. But if our way of life doesn't match up with our personal values, things feel wrong. This can cause deep unhappiness, which is why it is important to clearly identify values.

Values help us to make decisions, to know when to stand our ground and how to choose our friends. They give us a solid foundation to face the world. They can change throughout life as we learn new things or find ourselves in different circumstances.

Often we are not consciously aware of our values. Like beliefs, they can feel as if that's just how things should be. There are two reasons to make our values clear to ourselves: they strengthen us in all the ways mentioned above to know what guides us; and we can be more understanding of other people if we realize that they might hold different values to ours.

When you define your personal values, you discover what

is truly important to you. A good way to start doing this is to look back on your life so far — to identify when you felt really good, and really confident that you were making good choices. Think about each of the following questions, aiming to find the answers from your centre or 'from the heart'. Take into account both your career and your personal life in order to find balance in your answers.

When do you feel you are being true to yourself? When do you really feel like *you* are at your best?

When you were you at your happiest? What were you doing? Who were you with? What other factors contributed to your happiness?

When did you feel proud of yourself? Why was that? Were other people proud of you too?

When did you feel most fulfilled and satisfied? How did that experience give your life meaning? What need or desire was fulfilled? In what way was it meaningful?

———

Based on your feelings of integrity, happiness, pride and fulfilment, choose your top values. Can you narrow them down to your top three? This may feel challenging, and it's okay to take some time to ponder the answers to these questions. Your personal values are key to who you are and the kind of person you want to be.

Some of life's decisions require you to choose what you value most, perhaps weighing up two values that are both important to you. When there are many options, or when you are under pressure from others to take a particular course of action, it can be helpful and comforting to rely on your values for guidance. One way of looking at whether you are living up to your values is to consider how you use your time.

LIST YOUR VALUES

Take a few moments to make two lists. First, write down all the things that you do, beginning with what takes most of your time. For many this will be your work, either outside the home or caring for children and other work within the home, but you could also break this down into its different aspects. Keep writing your list until you have put down all the activities you do, including things you do only occasionally, roughly in order of the amount of time you spend on each one. This is your 'do' list.

Now write down what you care about, starting with what you care most for and so on down the list. Many people put 'family' at the top. Try to be specific; the big concepts such as 'peace', 'truth' and so on might not yield as much information as you need for this exercise. This is your 'values' list.

Compare the two lists. Do the things you care most about get most of your time and attention? Why? If you care greatly about physical health but are not putting any time into exercise or healthy eating, are you living up to your values? If 'family' comes first on your 'values' list, are you giving them the time you feel they deserve or doing the things they need? It may be that those long hours at work are for the family, but are there other ways to show them that you care about them?

Looking closely at your lists, see whether you can make changes in the way you spend your time so that it more accurately reflects your values. For example, if you put 'social justice' or 'the environment' on your 'values' list, consider joining a group that takes action on these subjects.

Talk to someone you trust about your values and ask for feedback on how they see you in this respect.

MINDFULNESS

This technique, borrowed from Buddhism and adapted to Western thinking, has become an important part of therapy in recent years. It is the antidote to operating on autopilot as we often do. You'll know what I mean if you have ever intended to pick up some shopping on your way home from work and have found yourself at your house without even noticing the shop as you passed it. There are so many routine activities we need to do each day that our mind saves energy by powering down to habits that take little thought or attention. In the process we lose the opportunity to be really awake and aware of our life. And while the mind is idling it easily switches to negative ruminations. Mindfulness gives us the opportunity to take control of our attention and to use it in our best interests.

There are some very simple ways to be mindful. Slow down. Do only one thing at a time and finish a task before starting another one. Drink a glass of water mindfully, noticing how it feels, how grateful your body is for its refreshment. Be a gentle, friendly observer of your actions, not trying to change or judge anything but kindly noticing.

Mindfulness means paying attention to what goes on in your mind, learning to be curious rather than frightened of it. This is easier than you might think. It can be done in two ways: by formally sitting down and focusing on your breath, body and thoughts, or by going about your day with clear attention on each task and each moment. We each have a constant chatter of thoughts and distractions running through our mind, time-travelling back and forth from the past to the future with only brief pauses in the present. That's how our brain works, continually making connections and sending out messages. It is not necessary (or even possible!) to empty the mind or silence the chatter. Mindfulness simply asks us to focus on the present moment and we can do that by observing what is going on.

The formal way to try this is to sit quietly, grounded in your body and taking note of your senses as you breathe. Try this for a few minutes when you know you won't be interrupted. Sit comfortably, upright with your back straight so that you can be relaxed but attentive. Slowly scan your body from feet to legs to torso to shoulders, from arms and neck to head and face. Notice the sensations in each part of the body without trying to change them or achieve anything in particular — just be aware. If there is no noticeable sensation in one part of your body, just notice that and move to the next part.

Once you have scanned the body, you could use a different sense, perhaps listening to all the sounds you can hear while sitting quietly. How many can you notice? Are there sounds within you as well as outside you? Can you hear sounds within the sounds? Don't judge what you hear, just notice what your ears are taking in.

Now turn your attention to your breath, noticing how it comes in and goes out. Feel your chest and abdomen gently rise and fall. Thoughts will arise and take hold of your attention from time to time. Don't criticize yourself for this; it is just what thoughts do. Let go of each thought and bring your attention back to the breath. This is the anchor for mindfulness. It can help to think 'Just this breath, just this breath' as each breath passes.

Start with just 1 minute of mindful sitting. You might find you can go on to another minute or even a few more. There is no set requirement; just beginning to be aware is enough. Doing this daily will begin your mindfulness practice.

There are many different guides to this exercise and you can find audio instructions on the internet or on CD. Some towns have mindfulness courses that give instruction and practice with the added benefit of being supported by a group and a tutor.

THE 3-MINUTE BREATHING SPACE[1]

Here is a simple version of an exercise to help you learn the basics of mindfulness.

- Sit or stand in an upright position.
- Ask, what is my experience right now? Notice any thoughts or feelings and any sensations in your body, as well as sounds from your environment.
- Now focus your attention on the sensations of breathing: the rise and fall of your abdomen, the feeling of the breath in your nostrils. Allow your attention to follow the breath all the way in and all the way out.
- Expand your attention to take in your breath and your whole body, including your posture and your facial expression.
- Explore any sensations or discomforts, breathing into them and accepting them without judging them, before moving your attention out again to an expanded awareness of the room or environment around you.
- This exercise can be done several times a day to centre and calm yourself.

For a more general experience of mindfulness, try to become more aware of your daily activities. While you are doing the dishes, notice the temperature of the water, the texture of each item you hold, the colours of the plates and cups. If you are driving, be aware of your surroundings and bring your thoughts back to the road, the traffic, the movements of driving, how relaxed your body can be in the car seat.

Whenever you notice you have been lost in thought for a while, come back to your surroundings and let your senses take in all the colours, sounds and smells that are going on right now. Look for the safety and peace that are part of the present moment. For just a few moments, as often as you can during the day, pay attention and be aware of where you are and what you are doing.

Now and then, change a regular activity slightly — use the opposite hand to clean your teeth, take a different route to work, go for a walk at a different time of day and let your attention and senses be brought to life. Shake up your habits a little to help you stay awake to your life.

GRATITUDE

Gratitude isn't only expressed in words. Sometimes the words 'thank you' are not even needed. In Nepal the nearest equivalent is used only for major obligations such as when someone has saved your life. It is understood that natural give and take will cover the day-to-day matters. The Japanese equivalent of grace before a meal translates as 'I will eat' but the gratitude is very plain in that simple phrase.

All spiritual traditions include gratitude in some form. We are taught to say prayers of thanks but a sense of gratitude goes beyond words into feelings of contentment or reverence, even awe. You don't need to be part of a formal religion to have an awareness of a bigger picture. Gratitude can help us to be humble and to recognize that we frequently get much more than we deserve. (In fact, deserving doesn't really come into it.)

In dark times, gratitude is the antidote to depression that says, 'It's hopeless, it will never work' and anxiety that says 'This is terrifying. How will I cope?' Gratitude says, 'There is enough, more than enough. Thank you. It will be all right.' Taking a moment to be consciously grateful allows us to appreciate and savour the good things that happen. In relationships with others, giving something back in words or actions creates connection. It is the social glue of community. Gratitude opens the heart and changes the point of view.

Each day, look for things to be grateful for. There are so many, from a hot shower in the morning to the convenience of boiling the kettle for a cup of tea, to the warm bed and interesting book (spare the author a thought for all that patient work!) before turning off the — so helpful! — bedside light. In between come all kinds of gifts: a smile from a stranger in the street, a work issue falling neatly into place, a phone call from someone who cares. Pondering a few of these gifts each day gives a sense of wellbeing.

You can also be grateful for aspects of yourself: your health, the strength of your body, your personality and skills. Sometimes the things you don't feel so grateful for can point to other attributes you can appreciate. 'I don't like my short, chunky legs' can become 'I'm grateful that I have strong legs and can enjoy walking in the hills.' 'I wish my father hadn't been so hard on me' could become 'I'm grateful for the work ethic I learnt in my family, which has helped me forge a good career.' There is always another aspect to be found, for which we can be grateful.

To stimulate feelings of gratitude, try asking yourself questions such as those listed below. Some people make this a daily practice, reflecting on and writing down some of the things that occurred during each day for which they are grateful.

- What energized me?
- What barrier did I overcome?
- What did others do for me?
- What inspired me?
- What made me feel good?
- What difficulty taught me an important lesson?

It might be the things that make life easier: hot water, electricity, the machines that help us do our work; or a fine day that makes the walk to work pleasant, a smile from a passer-by. Or it might be personal qualities: the ability to get on well with people, a good knowledge of maths, the strength to do physical work.

Gratitude is a mind state that leads to happiness and contentment. We can so easily get caught up in negative emotions about the past or future, such as resentment, anger or fear, but such emotions are destructive and painful for us as well as for others. Gratitude unsticks us from the cycle of craving and complaining and allows us to return to the present with all it has for us right here and now.

Remembering to be grateful is a good way to develop a positive and accepting attitude towards ourselves and others. Whenever you notice that your energy is negative, ask yourself: What am I grateful for?

COMPASSION

All the major religions emphasize the need to treat others as we would wish to be treated, and all recognize that it takes practice and discipline to do this consistently. Through compassion we can bring meaning and purpose to our life and develop wisdom. To do this we create an attitude of kindness to self and others.

Kristin Neff, who has written extensively about compassion, defines it like this:

> **First, to have compassion for others you must notice that they are suffering. If you ignore that homeless person on the street, you can't feel compassion for how difficult his or her experience is. Second, compassion involves feeling moved by others' suffering so that your heart responds to their pain (the word compassion literally means to 'suffer with'). When this occurs, you feel warmth, caring and the desire to help the suffering person in some way. Having compassion also means that you offer understanding and kindness to others when they fail or make mistakes, rather than judging them harshly. Finally, when you feel compassion for another (rather than mere pity), it means that you realize that suffering, failure and imperfection is part of the shared human experience.[2]**

A Buddhist monk, teaching on the subject of kindness, acknowledged that he, too, needs constant practice to maintain an attitude of kindness, even though he devotes his whole life to the subject and is not facing any threat or challenge. Compassion is an essential quality for living happily with others and at times it is in conflict with other drives, such as fear or achievement, making it necessary to consciously practise compassion towards ourselves and others.

A good place to start is by suspending judgment. We all arrive on the planet in circumstances we have not chosen, with no more idea of what is going on than we are given by our family and those who care for us when we are young. We all have to live with the knowledge that life is impermanent and some suffering is inevitable, so we all have at least this in common. It helps to understand that when people, ourselves included, behave 'badly' they are usually doing what they consider 'right' according to their model of the world.

Parents often comment on the pleasure they feel when viewing the world through their children's eyes, delighting in small joys as if they were completely new experiences. If you have the opportunity, try watching a young child approach life with no sense of judgment, just an openness and curiosity to accept what comes along and learn to work with it. As children grow older they take on board the judgments and assessments of others, until as teenagers they are consumed by trying to be who they think they should be in order to fit in with people with whom they think they should belong. They assemble a set of 'shoulds' to restrict and guide them. While some of this is necessary in order to fit in to society and be a co-operative member of the community, most people take it too far.

Each 'should' denies reality. The people in your life were who they were, the things you have done were what you could do at the time. The disappointment gap between the ideal and what is really happening gnaws at confidence and takes the gloss off the very real joys of day-to-day life.

Sometimes people are surprised to learn that their judgments, like their beliefs, are things they have built up over time and are not actual facts. As I mentioned under 'beliefs' in the previous chapter, these 'rules' for life have usually been assembled at a very young age. Think how much you have learnt and experienced since you were a child — surely it's worth revising your views from time to time.

This approach includes self-judgment. Accept that you are doing your best and will do better when you can, give yourself credit for successes and set realistic goals. As Kristin Neff puts it, try to look at your own suffering with kindness and caring, and realize that you are not alone: suffering and imperfection are part of life. Treat yourself as you would treat a good friend.

Suspending judgment leads to acceptance — of how things actually are, rather than how we want them to be. This is another way of being in the present, alert and aware. It's a great basis for developing compassion.

When you feel bowed down by depression, amid feelings of guilt and failure, you might find it hard to be kind to yourself, let alone others. You may wish that someone would be kind to you, even comfort and care for you. But the only person any of us can change is ourselves. Then, sometimes, others will change in response to our new behaviour.

Keep coming back to thoughts of warmth and kindness towards yourself, even if you can only do this for short periods of time. Maybe you can capture the feeling by thinking of someone, or even a pet, who loves you and responds warmly to you.

Some people find it helpful to use a mantra or short prayer. There is a Buddhist one that goes, 'May I [they, you] be safe and free from suffering. May I be as happy and as healthy as it is possible to be. May I have ease of being.' Try going through these phrases, thinking of yourself, those you love, people you are aware of but not close to, the world at large.

If you have been able to practise some of the suggestions above and are beginning to treat yourself more compassionately, look around for something you can care about. It could be a plant or a pet, a friend who would appreciate your time and your kindness, or a cause you could support.

Kindness is a two-way street. When we treat others kindly, we feel a sense of wellbeing. It is part of the social nature of human beings that we experience meaning and purpose in connecting with others.

CREATIVITY

Some may think that creativity is for talented artists, writers or musicians, but we each have it in us. Perhaps because nature is in a constant state of creation, and because we are part of nature, creativity is an essential part of life. It can certainly make a significant contribution to wellbeing. We don't have to be 'successful' in our creative endeavours, and many of them, such as journalling or sketching or singing in the shower, might never be shared.

Cooking a meal, tending a garden, arranging the furnishings, building a set of shelves or constructing a model plane: these are all creative acts. You might notice that when you do something like this you get absorbed in the process and lose the sense of time passing. This is one of the great benefits of creativity. It allows us to be very attentive to the present moment.

For some lucky people their work is clearly creative. An engineer designs, draws and solves problems to make machinery that is a very visible and functional creation. A violinist in an orchestra or a dancer in the ballet each have jobs we have no trouble defining as creative. But almost everything is creative in some way. A builder's labourer who is digging holes for foundations is contributing to the building. A mother making the twentieth meal this week for her family is being creative — perhaps cleverly so with what's left in the fridge!

We may need a little more creativity in our lives, however, beyond the day-to-day things we do. Think about what you enjoy and try to give yourself some time to develop it. It might be journalling to record your thoughts and observations of your life, or scrapbooking, making something in the shed or creating a garden or some pot plants if you have the space. You can do it in whatever way suits you. Having a perfect result is not the purpose; it is more important to be playful and absorbed in the process.

The 100 Days Project invites people to commit to doing one activity every day for 100 days, with the focus on process. Check out the website http://100daysproject.co.nz/ and see what others have done. It may inspire you.

CONNECTION

Being mindful, grateful, compassionate and awake will naturally bring connection with the present moment, with nature and with others.

Connection with nature can be felt in a natural environment: walking in a garden, a park, the hills or on a beach. Sit under a tree and look up through the branches or watch the clouds move across the sky. A few moments spent like this can be calming. If you can take a whole day out in the natural world, perhaps hiking or paddling a canoe, stress can fall away.

Animals can show you how to live in the moment and to truly relax between bursts of activities. Birds in a garden or forest charm us with their graceful movements and lovely song as well as that enviable ability to fly.

Farm animals have a social life that is intriguing to observe. Watching fish in a tank or a pond can also help us relax. Finding a way to connect with nature reminds us that we are part of the natural world in which processes are working as they should and the cycle of life carries on whether or not we are worrying and striving. A sense of being part of the bigger picture can, at its miraculous best, be a deeply spiritual experience. In an everyday, simple way it can be relaxing and comforting.

Connecting with other human beings is essential for us because we are social creatures whose brain has developed to interact and remember others, filing away their personal details and other relationships. One way to stave off dementia is to meet new people and keep our brains active in this way.

In order to make connections with people we need to reach out and speak with them. In a small way this can happen by greeting the people we see in our daily routine and exchanging a sentence or two. A comment about the weather as you check out your groceries can be a very easy way of finding common ground because we are all experiencing the same thing: 'Cold, isn't it?' 'Do you think it will rain?' It's a cliché but can be a friendly one.

To take the connection a step further, try to remember some small thing about the people you see regularly. How is the shopkeeper's son getting on at university? Did your colleague go fishing on the weekend as she had planned?

Closer connections come from spending longer together and having more detailed conversations. Share your feelings with someone you trust. Talk about your hopes and dreams with your partner. Plan activities together and enjoy the shared experience both at the time and recalling it later.

Be able to accept help. If you confide in a close friend, they may want to do something to show they care. Be willing to accept their offer gracefully — it will give them an opportunity to connect with you and you a chance to experience gratitude. Stay alert to what others might need of you and be willing to help them too, whether to directly reciprocate to someone who helped you or to 'pay it forward' to someone else in need.

Nurture important relationships. What does the person close to you need to thrive? Time, attention, good listening and feedback help to show that they are understood and cared about. Contact family and friends for a chat or to do something together. Don't always wait for others to make the call, even if you feel a bit diffident about reaching out. Even if they are not available to do what you suggest, most people appreciate being thought of.

There are many ways to feel connected and helpful through online petitions and groups, but also look for ways to be involved face-to-face if you can. Be active in your community. Our busy lives often make it difficult to take part in activities outside of work and family life, but think about where you could contribute. Does your church group need someone on the tea roster or to wash up afterwards? Could you get involved with your children's sports by joining the committee, helping with the fundraiser or driving some children who need transport to the game?

Find ways to give back, not to the detriment of your own

wellbeing or the time you need to give to yourself and your family, but in ways that will connect you to the people around you and benefit others as well as you.

MENDING RELATIONSHIPS

Depression can be hard on relationships, whether because of the inwardness that is part of depression or the tendency to become easily irritated or angry.

A traditional explanation of depression is that it is caused by anger turned inward, and for some people this is the case. All that bottling up and trying to be nice can lead you to feel that your thoughts and opinions are not very important, that others always come first. Here comes that defeat posture again, coupled with resentment — a toxic combination!

If this is what is happening to you, it is important to learn to speak your mind, resisting the negative voice that says, 'What's the use? No one listens to me' and finding a way to be heard. A lot has been written over the years about being assertive, which is a middle way between aggression (demanding) and submissiveness (giving in or giving up). Being able to express your opinion and ask for your needs to be met is an essential skill in adult life, one that is taught in tiny daily increments in supportive families and schools.

Anger can be a symptom of depression, perhaps because depression lowers resilience and makes a short fuse more likely. A tendency to self-medicate with alcohol will also contribute to anger by lessening self-control. If you are using alcohol with your antidepressants you may be undermining the effect of the medication since alcohol itself has a depressing effect. Check with your doctor. (See 'Do I have an addiction?' on page 151.)

If getting angry is a significant part of your depression you will need to make a choice. Remembering that anger is often caused by a gap between expectations and reality, you can do the following two things:

1. Accept the disappointment and let it go. This is different from bottling up your feelings, in that it involves truly accepting the situation and adapting yourself to it. It might mean lowering your expectations for the future. If you still have some residual anger, use exercise to disperse it.

2. Ask for your expectations to be met. This will involve some thought about what it really is that you want and whether the other person involved can deliver.

Fear often lies behind anger: fear of losing the one you love or fear of being put down and not listened to. Take some time to think about what it is for you and how you could address that. It is all too easy to get into the habit of losing your temper; if that is what has been happening, seek out someone to talk to, someone whose advice and wisdom you can trust.

If you choose to avert anger by asking for your expectations to be met, you could try a conflict-resolution process involving the following seven steps:

1. Ask the other person if they are willing to talk about the problem. If necessary, motivate them by explaining that you feel it is important to resolve the conflict in order to take care of your relationship/friendship/ability to work together.

2. Define what the problem is, either together or by taking turns to outline it.

3. Together, brainstorm as many solutions as you can. Think laterally and don't judge the solutions at this point. This step can be creative, even playful and fun.

4. Each rate the solutions according to preference.

5. Choose one that you can both agree on.

6. Try it for an agreed time.

7. Evaluate how it is working and if necessary start the process again.

FORGIVENESS

Sometimes it is not possible to sort things out with the people with whom you feel angry. They might not be willing to talk about it with you, or they may not be around to do it. Maybe they have died. To get past your anger it may be helpful to write a letter that expresses the way you feel — then tear it up or burn it to show that it's over. Or speak out loud to an empty chair, a photo or some other object that represents the person. When you have expressed everything you feel about what the person did that hurt you, and what you wish they had done instead, finish up with a statement that hands it back to the other person. Something like: 'But you didn't do what I wanted and now I'm letting go of the expectation that you should have.'

You may have to go through the process a few times but it can be very freeing to let go of an old hurt. Forgiving doesn't mean that you think it was okay for the person to hurt you, just that you don't want to hold on to it any longer.

We all have things we need to forgive ourselves for, too. If you are troubled by regret for things you did in the past, go through a process of forgiving yourself just as you would for someone else. Whatever has happened, we all need to learn the lesson, let go and come back to living in the present.

The exercise below provides a process for finding forgiveness. The final step is to send unconditional love to the person who needs forgiveness. If that seems too much for you right now, just think about letting go of your anger and hurt and leaving the responsibility for wrong-doing with the other person. If you are forgiving yourself, do your best to be loving towards yourself, perhaps by recalling the feeling you had when someone else treated you kindly or the feeling you have when you care for someone or something.

FORGIVENESS EXERCISE

Take a few moments when you know you won't be interrupted. At each step speak out loud, creating your own personal account by giving the details that are relevant for you.

Step 1. 'I choose to stop hurting myself for what [name of person] has done [or is doing].'

Step 2. Address the person in your imagination — use a chair, cushion or coloured cloth to represent the person: 'What you did made me feel _____. I would have preferred that you had said or done _____.'

Step 3. 'But you didn't do that. I don't want to hurt myself any more for what you have done. I'm tired of the discomfort I get from all this. I want to finish this now. I choose to heal this and let it go completely. I am choosing to be free of it.'

Step 4. 'I would have preferred that you had _____, but you didn't do that and I cancel that expectation.' (Repeat this for all expectations held.) 'I cancel all demands, expectations and conditions that you do [or say or be] what I would have preferred in the past and now. I cancel the demand that you be any certain way. You are totally responsible for your actions. I give that responsibility back to you now [gesture], and I release you now to your own good.'

Step 5. Close your eyes and raise your consciousness to the higher self. Imagine the love that the higher self has for you. Feel that compassion and love from the higher self; allow it to flow into you and release all the demands, conditions and expectations. Really feel the positive qualities of the higher self, that part of you that has protected you, loved you and nurtured you all the days of your life.

Step 6. With eyes still closed, continue to feel the love from the higher self and now say to the person you are forgiving: 'I send this love out from my higher self to you just as you are and have been, and I release you to your highest good.' Feel this love flowing out from you to this person. Take your time to feel and experience this.

Step 7. Now be aware of your body and how it feels.

Are you still holding on to any demands that this person change in any way? If you do not feel release, repeat the process for each action you are holding against this person. Always examine your willingness to be free. If it feels blocked, ask yourself: 'Is something else blocking this process?' Usually an answer will come to you quickly, and you can start to process it. When you have done what you can, feel deep gratitude that you can feel love from your higher self and can send it out to the forgiven one. The relief will come.

This exercise can be done often — for small hurts and for deep emotional trauma. It works any time we feel that love is blocked. Repetition begins to make it second nature — a good habit, like washing the dishes or cleaning your teeth!

JOURNALLING IN WORDS AND PICTURES

A creative way to bring all these points together is to keep a journal. Journalling is more than a record of each day's events or a list of appointments such as you might write in a diary. It can be a meaningful way to reflect on life and communicate with your deeper self.

Research has shown that journalling has physical and mental benefits that include an improved immune response as well as reduced anxiety.[3]

Find a notebook that you will enjoy using, selecting a format that works for you. Some people like small, compact journals, others prefer a larger page with plenty of space for drawing or collage. Some people use their computer or phone, but I prefer the physical feeling of hand-writing and sketching. Working by hand slows the process down. Try writing or drawing as slowly as you can and see what comes through.

An important aspect of journalling is that it is private. Ask family to respect your privacy and don't feel you have to share your journal with anyone. This is your space. After you have made your record and thought about it, you might want to talk about what you observe or to share an experience, but the journal is where you discover and process what is important to you. If you are sure that what you write or draw is private, you can feel free to be honest and will gain much more from the ability to be really in touch with your feelings and aware of your experience.

Take a few minutes daily or as often as you can to put your thoughts and feelings on the page. It can become like talking with a close friend. As thoughts come to you during the day, rather than ruminating and worrying, you can make a mental note that you will put those thoughts in your journal, perhaps even planning how you will do that. Make sure you note positive experiences, however small, and things you can be grateful for. If you find you have covered a problem in detail, don't stop until you have listed some solutions you can take responsibility for.

Be creative. If you are not confident in your drawing skills, that really doesn't matter. You can sketch stick figures or items that reflect your thoughts, or you can use colour to indicate different moods without needing to represent anything tangible. Stickers and cut-out pictures from magazines can create a collage. Glue in bus or movie tickets that will remind you of an outing, or anything that has a colour you like. Don't be afraid to be messy. The same goes for what you choose to write. Spelling, grammar and handwriting don't matter at all. Use lists or mind maps.

Journalling can help you put feelings such as anxiety into perspective. It can keep you focused on what you really want in life. It can create a sense of positive connection out of moments of solitude and let you value your time alone with your thoughts. It can help you catch and develop creative ideas and realize your dreams.

Tips for starting journalling:

- Get a notebook you will value.
- Keep it private.
- Start small — 10 minutes per day; just make some marks on the page.
- Allow yourself to be messy!
- Just try it.

HOW THEY GOT ON

Let's turn again to the people we've been following and see how they're going.

Laura

I talked with Dave and realized I'd been feeling really bitter towards my parents, blaming them for my depression. They live in a different town but I started phoning them and talking to them about the children and they were really grateful to be in touch again. I thought about how they did their best the way they saw it at the time and how they have mellowed as they've gotten older, and it made me think about how things change in life. I wouldn't go back to church, it was too judgmental and not good for my personality, but it did give me some ideas about the bigger picture. Sometimes Dave and I have long talks about the meaning of life and how we see it. I enjoy that and it brings us closer.

Jackson

After a while I realized I was hanging out with my parents more, which was nice but a bit soft, so I started talking to this one guy at school I thought was okay. We went out on the mountain bike tracks sometimes and I went to his place to see some new gear he had and watch some rides on YouTube. It occurred to me that I hadn't cried for a couple of months, so that felt good.

When my brother came home from uni I talked to him. It was good to feel not so alone. He's a bit blunt. He said you can't just curl up and die in a corner, you have to keep going and you will get through. He said he was terrified when he went to uni but it got better. I was surprised to find even the star had bad times.

Josie

The counsellor got me to do this values exercise, putting cards in order to show what I thought was important in life. I hadn't really thought about it like that and it was hard to do, but I can see how good it is to know what you stand for. I also started doing some art. I'm not that good but it's fun and I can get lost in it for an hour or more, especially if I put music on at the same time. I have a friend now too, and we hang out together at school and sometimes on the weekend.

Tom

Sally and I are getting on better than we have in years. I apologized to her for being such a workaholic when the kids were growing up and she was quite decent about it. I see now that there are more important things than how hard I work, but it was all I knew at the time. Sometimes, when I'm potting seedlings in the nursery tunnel house and the sun comes through and lights up all my little fresh plants, I feel really happy. Funny that.

Kathy

I accept that I have a tendency to depression and will probably need medication throughout my life. Recently someone was talking about how it's genetic and it certainly seems that way. But while I've been on the medication I have changed a lot about how I see myself and the world in general. I feel more connected to my husband and children and I can enjoy things like a walk in the hills or listening to music. Sometimes I tear up but in a good way, at something beautiful or brave that moves me. It's a surprising feeling.

8.

RESILIENCE

Resilience is the ability to face challenges and recover from hard times. It's about having something in reserve to meet any extra demands and having back-up from the people around us. Life can be unpredictable in its ups and downs. Becoming resilient gives us a better chance of responding well to whatever we are called upon to cope with.

Taking care of ourselves in all areas — body, mind and spirit — fosters resilience. It's getting fit for whatever life might deliver. Experiences that encourage us to learn new skills and to test ourselves will develop resilience, which is needed to prevent a recurrence of depression or to make it easier to cope with if it does return.

If you have read the previous chapters and tried out some of the suggestions, you have already been building resilience. Chapters 5, 6 and 7 offer a physical and mental fitness program that will prepare you to meet life's challenges.

Here are some tips specific to this important skill.

KNOW YOUR STRENGTHS

When the pressure is on it is all too easy to underestimate yourself and feel overwhelmed. Think about your strengths and perhaps ask a trusted friend or family member to give you feedback. (Don't wait for a crisis — this is useful at any time!) Look for the positives. You might think of yourself as unassertive but on the positive side this could mean that you are humble and willing to help others.

Can you recall times when you used your strengths to cope with a situation? For example, the skill of learning to drive requires patience, persistence and the courage to face the examiner on the day of your test. Starting a new job or a new school takes bravery as well as the ability to be friendly and connect with others.

Learning to swim was a big challenge for me and at times it felt frustrating, impossible even. However, I am very persistent and like to see things through, so I knew these strengths were on my side, but I also needed to apply self-compassion in order to manage my disappointment when my progress was very slow and I was way behind the others in the group.

BUILD YOUR STRENGTHS

List your strengths and put the list where you can see it often. Choose some that you would like to develop and every now and then make that skill a focus for the day. Use your journal to record times when you used courage or perseverance or self-compassion during the day. If you are working on a skill that you feel needs to be nurtured and strengthened, can you list some times in the past when you have used this skill? Is there someone who could be a role model or mentor for you and this skill?

REALITY CHECK

Our emotional brain is often too quick to panic and assume the worst. Psychologists call it catastrophizing. Folk wisdom calls it making mountains out of molehills! Tune in your rational, analytic brain and ask, is this really a disaster? Using a scale from one to ten, if ten is the worst thing that could happen, such as severe injury or the death of a loved one, and one is cruisy with no problems, where would you rate this situation?

In my case, swimming slowly up the pool, even if I was a full lap behind my classmates, was not a disaster although I felt panicky about it. In fact, if I rated it honestly, it was a positive not a negative because I could at least swim the full length of the pool. Certainly nobody died! Getting the situation into perspective is a great boost for resilience as we realize, phew, this is not really a threat. From there you can move to 'I can handle this'.

Look out for words such as 'always' and 'never', which indicate you could be catastrophizing, i.e. thinking the worst. 'I'm *always* last, I'll *never* improve' are not only not true, they are not helpful or kind to yourself.

In the same way, be aware that problems don't last forever. Time brings changes. Remind yourself, 'I can get through this. It's short term in the scheme of my life.'

I love my swimming now and even though I'm still slower than many others, I can enjoy moving steadily in the water, feeling strong and capable, knowing that I developed this skill through patience and persistence, with a little self-compassion.

To help your sense of perspective, name the problem clearly and decide how much control you have over it. Is it even necessary to be involved in this problem? It's easy to be annoyed with work that is poorly done or people who break the rules, but are you responsible here? Sometimes it's best to take note of what the problem is and how you feel and then let it go. If you do your part, according to your standards and values, it's up to others to do theirs and if they don't, unless you are their boss or the police, it's not your problem. Realizing this and letting go can be a big relief.

CREDIT WHERE IT'S DUE

Celebrate successes and enlist others to join you in feeling good about whatever you achieve. Enjoy your moment in the sun before setting the next goal. Research has shown that learning to savour success develops resilience through feeling good and being aware of doing well.[1]

There is a sense of satisfaction that comes with learning a skill or completing a task well. We call this mastery and it can come into all kinds of situations. I have watched my grandsons throw stones into water over and over, delighting at the longest throw, the most accurate one, then moving on to making the stone skip. They are a little competitive but mainly they focus on improving their own skill. They can do this for a long time, learning how to use their bodies to the best effect and recently the younger one (aged five) kindly offered to show me how. The sense of satisfaction in having a skill and being able to share it was very clear. Feelings of mastery last longer than happiness. Happiness is better thought of as an outcome of mastery or success, rather than a goal in itself.

Here are some key points for savouring the good times and making sure they are embedded in your memory so that they become part of your sense of yourself.

- Share your successes with others. This isn't boasting; you can talk about your good fortune without making it sound like point-scoring. Also, those close to you will know you are quick to be pleased about others' good fortune in return. Tell your family and friends about completing a project, sticking to your health goals for a whole month, getting a promotion at work. Let them be happy for you.

- Build the memory. Don't be too hasty in moving on to the next goal or looking for the flaw that could be improved on. Let the success sink in and notice all its aspects: how it looked, felt, tasted and smelt if those are relevant. Really take note of this moment in time.
- Congratulate yourself. Yes, it's all right to feel proud of yourself and say, 'well done!'
- Allow yourself to become absorbed in your task. 'Flow' describes the feeling of losing your sense of time and your self-consciousness to become one with an activity. Creative people talk about flow (which some people refer to as 'being in the zone'), as do those devoted to a sport. It's a powerful feeling of being in the moment and being effective.
- Sharpen your perception and allow your senses to bring you all the information that's available for the activity.
- Count your blessings and be grateful.
- Be realistic in making comparisons: there will always be others who are better at a skill than you are, just as you will always be better than some.

Psychologist and author Rick Hanson talks about allowing your mammalian brain — the part of you that is geared to seek rewards — to feel satisfied. He calls this process 'feeding the mouse' and suggests that in day-to-day life we make the most of opportunities to feel 'fed'. He describes a range of experiences that meet this need, from the pleasures of our senses to the achievement of our goals, from the natural world around us to the wonders of human technology. Throughout every day, good things come to us if only we notice and appreciate them. Make sure you spend some time being aware of what you have. A good time for this, Hanson suggests, can be just before bed. Think about how you have had enough food to eat, how you completed some tasks that day, and the love of friends and family. Let yourself really feel the good in your life.[2]

LOOK ON THE BRIGHT SIDE

Some would say that it's naïve to see the bright side, but often the doom and gloom we gather comes from the negativity bias that is in us all, as a driver to keep us safe. Look around objectively. Are you safe? Then don't keep thinking the worst. That negativity bias also drives our news media, because disaster, trauma and danger attract attention and feed the ratings ('If it bleeds, it leads' is an old journalists' maxim).

You would never know it from the evening news, but the world is actually getting better in many ways. Fewer people are hungry, people are better educated and there is greater awareness of the need to care for the environment. In most countries the crime rate is falling and life expectancy is rising. Fewer people die in wars. If this surprises you, you might be taking the news media too seriously.[3]

When the information you get through the media overwhelms you with hopelessness, ration your intake of current affairs. Some people take a holiday from news media altogether. It's a bit like going gluten-free: 'I find the news just doesn't agree with me. I feel so much better since I gave it up.'

If going news-free seems irresponsible or isolating to you, try to reduce the number of platforms and times each day that you imbibe the news. For example, check the headlines online in the morning, then give it a rest. You could finish the day with a radio round-up while you commute home, then focus on the present and find the safety that is part of your own life.

Worrying about others who are not part of your own life will not save them. You could use your concern to donate to or volunteer with an appropriate organization, but lying awake at night with a feeling of global dread helps no one, certainly not you.

Paying attention to friends and family will improve your sense of wellbeing. Divert some of the time you spend on the news to talking, exercising or playing a game with a friend or family member. Take a break from all media in order to relax before going to bed. You'll sleep much better (see Chapter 5, pages 54–58, on sleep).

The same goes for social media. If you find your use of social media is creating stress or a low mood, ration it. Decide which aspects are causing you pain and limit them. It's fine to block some inputs and not read comments that often show people at their worst. (If cute animal videos lift your mood, leave them in!) We need face-to-face time with the people in our lives in order to settle our emotions and feel a sense of belonging. At its best, social media is only a thin substitute for this.

FIND COMMUNITY, NURTURE FAMILY

Human beings are social creatures; we do best in supportive groups. If you can, join a group that shares your interests and values. This will be hard to do when depression has a hold on you, but as you recover, pay attention to this need for community. It will improve your resilience and help prevent a recurrence of depression. Local newspapers or online groups will have contact details for all kinds of activities.

If there is no group that appeals to you or feels approachable, form your own group. Look for others who you can feel on board with and, if possible, some you look up to. We become like the people we hang out with, so choose people you would like to be like! Pick an activity with a little striving in it. Meet regularly. Food often provides a focus for the social part of a session and even if you feel too shy to join in the conversation, sitting with others to eat and drink and listening to the chat can create a good feeling.

There are all kinds of informal groups who carry out some activity then socialize together. An example is a cycling group who have a weekly ride, followed by coffee at a favourite café. Or a book group who meet over tea and cake to discuss new and maybe challenging literature. Or community gardeners who cultivate vegetables together on an allotment or weed and nurture a public park, then sit down with a thermos and biscuits for a chat. The winning formula is a little effort on a task of shared interest, then some social time, perhaps with food and drink. Be a little cautious if the activity ends up in the pub — remember, alcohol is not your friend while you are managing depression.

Our resilience is often developed in connection with others. Find your allies and bring them into your plans and endeavours. Avoid the nay-sayers and doom merchants if you can. If you can't, try not to take them too seriously.

Family is a natural group and at its best it provides love, safety and support. I acknowledge that for some, family has proved to be unsafe either mentally or physically and needs to be avoided. However, unless that is the case, it is important to take care of our family relationships.

Children who have siblings they are close to are generally more resilient, whether the siblings are older or younger. The intense connection of brothers and sisters provides a great opportunity to learn how to manage relationships, for example, through accepting one another for who they are and by developing conflict resolution skills, because avoidance won't work in family life. Many siblings talk about the love–hate relationships they have and acknowledge that in spite of great frustration and provocation there is a strong sense of someone who will always be there. At their best, when the pressure is on, siblings have each other's backs. Older children develop important skills when they care for younger children. The important factor is to have a sense of being known and accepted by the other.

These relationships are vital for children as they grow up, but as adults do we still appreciate them? In adult life siblings often drift apart, coming together only for the big family occasions of weddings and funerals. If you have a brother or sister or perhaps a cousin who cares about you, can you nurture that relationship? Phone calls to keep in touch, visits, remembering special occasions such as birthdays or children's special events, show we value the relationship and keep the other in mind.

Not everyone has a close brother or sister, and in some cases those sibling relationships are risky or even abusive. Other types of connection can also build resilience: a close friend, a teacher or someone from the extended family such as a grandparent or an aunt. For many, a pet is a constant, unconditional companion. Needing to take care of another living being grows inner strength and dependability. Keeping in touch with people who are important to us not only gives a warm feeling of being connected, but it can also provide a network for back-up when times are hard. Don't forget, you are part of their network too. Be sure to reach out when someone in your family or friendship group needs support.

MEANING

Everyone wants to avoid pain and seek happiness. This is natural, but the way we define happiness varies widely from one culture to another. For many, happiness means success: a good job with status that others respect, a successful relationship, a comfortable home and all the things society values. But chasing that kind of happiness is like getting a sugar high that comes and goes all too quickly. It is possible to have the things society deems desirable and still feel empty and unfulfilled.

A more lasting sense of satisfaction comes from having meaning in life. Emily Esfahani Smith studied positive psychology and travelled the United States interviewing a range of people to discover what makes life worthwhile.[4] She distilled their answers into what she named the Four Pillars of Meaning: belonging, purpose, transcendence and storytelling.

1. Belonging

People who feel connected to others — family, community, school or church groups — generally find life worth living. True belonging comes from being accepted by the group because of who you are, not just for what you believe or the rules you follow. Love is the basis of this powerful sense of connection, even in the small interactions of daily life. The key is to see the other person as they are and to relate openly, even in a simple transaction such as getting on a bus or buying a coffee.

Many people have described using thoughts of those they love to get them through hard times. Some of these accounts show tremendous courage in the face of terrible events.[5] Emily describes how her father used his children's names as a mantra when about to undergo surgery.

2. Purpose

People who have found their calling have a sense of purpose in their lives. This comes from using your strengths to serve others and could range from making a loved one's favourite dinner to managing a philanthropic organization. Start small. Sometimes we are distracted from seeing the possibilities in our own lives by looking at the work of people who we admire but would find hard to emulate. We can't all be Nelson Mandela or Mother Teresa but we can all use our skills to show love to others. When I returned to work after my children started school, a kind friend cleaned my house every Friday. She would finish by polishing the table and picking some flowers from the garden to put in a vase. It was a delight to come home to the smell of furniture polish and the flowers in the centre of the table and to know that the weekend would be a time for me and the children, without having to worry about housework. I remember it still, many years later.

What can you do today that will reach out to someone else?

3. Transcendence

Transcendence involves getting into a mental state of complete focus and engagement. 'Flow', as discussed on page 137, is the word for losing ourselves in an activity. In a flow state we can become so absorbed in what we are doing that when we pause, we find that time has passed without our being aware of it. We can all find that feeling in something that takes up our whole attention.

Another aspect of transcendence is the sense of being part of something bigger than ourselves. This can be found in nature — look up into the branches of a tall tree for a few minutes and notice a sense of perspective develop. Observe the sea, a river or the sky. Feeling part of something beyond ourselves is also a key aspect of spiritual practice, as long as the practice is consistent with our values and who we are.

4. Storytelling

We all tell the 'story' of our lives, creating memories and an understanding of how we became ourselves. The stories we create can be disempowering or encouraging. We can change and reinterpret the way we tell ourselves about our lives, even while we are limited by the facts. For example, someone who suffered deep grief from the loss of a relationship she had held hope in, can in time see that loss as a turning point that helped her to understand herself better and eventually form a new relationship, better suited to her best self.

Telling the story of our lives, to ourselves or others, is an important factor in creating our sense of identity. Try writing a short account of your life in your journal. Perhaps write the sad version and then the resilient story. Notice what you select to make each account and how reading it through makes you feel.

Dan Gilbert, in his 2004 TED talk, offers some creative research that demonstrates how we convince ourselves of our happiness or unhappiness, quite apart from the facts of our lives. People who are the happiest are often the ones who have the least choice in life — they are making the best of things as they find them. We are very poor predictors of how happy we will be if we get the things we desire most, or of how lasting the happiness from a major success, such as winning the lottery or finding the perfect mate, will actually be. (Most people return to their previous state in a few months.)

Gilbert refers to our 'psychological immune system', the ability to protect ourselves from adversity purely through the way we think. He credits a major evolutionary development of the brain, the prefrontal cortex, which our primate ancestors did not have. This part of our brain allows us to simulate experiences. He gives the example that you don't need to try liver and onion ice-cream to know it is 'yuck!' — simply imagining it is enough!

The skill of simulation allows us to experience the best and worst of scenarios and prepare for them. But it can misfire. We tend to exaggerate how good the best can be, leading to envy of others or frustration that what we desire is out of reach. We also over-predict danger and create imaginary fears, believing that we will not cope, when in fact we may be more resilient than we realize.

It is through storytelling that we can actively choose to be content. As Shakespeare put it: 'There is nothing either good or bad, but thinking makes it so.'[6]

MANAGING OBSTACLES

At times you will fail.

I am not being pessimistic here. Everyone will fail at something, sometime. If you know that failure is part of the process, you can avoid the mistake of thinking that you 'won't' or 'shouldn't' fail. This makes it more likely that you can prepare yourself for any predictable obstacles and work out how to overcome them. Accepting failure as part of the process can help you to learn from setbacks and avoid judging or criticising yourself for them.

Resilient people see setbacks as separate from themselves, problems to be solved rather than character flaws. Not 'I can't do this, I'm useless' but 'How can I do this? Which of my skills do I need here?' Or 'How can I learn how to do this? Who can advise me? Where will I find the necessary information?'

Gabrielle Oettingen uses the acronym WOOP:

- **Wish:** what is your deepest wish?
- **Outcome:** how would you like things to turn out?
- **Obstacles:** what could get in the way?
- **Plan:** what steps can you create to move towards your wish, taking the obstacles into account?[7]

For example: 'I wish to see my sister. The outcome I want is to travel to the city she lives in at the other end of the country. Obstacles are the cost of the airfare, getting time off work, being sure that she has time to host me and dealing with my responsibilities at home. The plan: contact my sister and see when it would suit her, look at my budget and see where I could save towards the visit, watch airlines for cheap fares, talk to my boss about taking time off, ask a friend to feed the cat. By thinking ahead and working towards a time in the future that suits everyone, the plan could work.'

Simply believing 'you can do it' is not enough if you don't yet have the skills or all the information. Exercises in visualizing the goal already achieved can trick us into becoming complacent. When we imagine we've reached the goal, our brain perceives this as 'job done!' and goes into a relaxed state. This can stop us making the effort to achieve a goal.

Oettingen recommends being mindful not just of our desires, but also of the barriers that we or the world might place in their way. We can then make realistic plans that include steps to overcome or work around the obstacles. Her research shows that this is a more effective way of achieving our goals.

RELAPSE

Even when we think we have anticipated and planned for the obstacles that might come up, setbacks will occur. Managing setbacks means picking yourself up and getting back on track. The catastrophizing response is to think, 'This is hopeless' and give up. The resilient response is to think, 'Well, that didn't work. How can I do it better?'

Depression will almost inevitably make a comeback. Perhaps you feel well for a period of time and lighten up on the routine that you established in Chapter 5. Maybe you have a few late nights, drink a bit more alcohol, lose out on time for yourself. That's fine while you are still doing well, but giving up on self-care will eventually have consequences. A grey day is not a message that you have failed miserably, just a reminder that self-care is needed once again.

Take stock and find out what might be missing. Do you need a few early nights? An afternoon on the weekend where you do something you love rather than rush around doing what others want of you? Can you make your diet healthier? Or is there something on your mind that you need to talk over with a trusted friend? Taking time out to consider all the factors will give you the opportunity to make the necessary adjustments.

In the end there is no failure, only information. The best response is to keep getting back on track, patiently, without judgment or criticism. If possible, find an ally who will remind you of this on a bad day and help you discover the best steps to recovery. This could be a trusted friend or family member, or a counsellor, psychologist or coach.

BE SAFE

As I write this, a series of high-profile scandals has shocked the Western world. This is nothing new. Many of us were already aware of the abuse of power in all kinds of settings, from family life to public life. While sexual abuse in settings such as the entertainment world or political life are newsworthy and shocking, domestic abuse and workplace bullying go on daily, often unreported. Too many people suffer in their day-to-day lives without seeing a way out.

Being trapped in an abusive situation will set anyone up for depression. The factors of helplessness, ongoing suffering that cannot be avoided and the experience of being so undervalued and disrespected as to be made a victim are strong precursors for depression.

We all want to avoid harm and maximize the good in life. People do not stay in harmful situations because they want to. Often the harm is difficult to define and better options hard to see. Many people find it hard to decide where to draw the line, especially if their partner is remorseful or blames outside influences such as work stress or alcohol. This can be made even more difficult when you are depressed and do not have the emotional resources or self-esteem to see there might be better options. It is really important to get another perspective on the situation, from a trusted friend or family member or from a counsellor, doctor or other professional.

Emotional abuse, where the perpetrator uses mind games and put-downs as a means of control, is even harder to be clear about. Many women, especially, want to think the best of others and can be very forgiving, at a cost to their own wellbeing. But men, too, are subjected to domestic abuse and workplace bullying and may feel too ashamed to ask for help.

You have a right to feel safe and respected, at home, at work and in the public space. A situation that makes you feel that you count for very little in another person's eyes will cause and maintain depression. Seek help. There are organizations with a good understanding of the dynamics of abuse and trained staff or volunteers who will offer support. Talking about your situation with one or two trusted people will help you gain perspective. If the advice you receive feels wrong, talk to a few more people. Ultimately you are the expert on your situation and what is best for you.

———

Resilience is a complex subject because it is woven into all aspects of life and everyone's life is different. You will develop your own resilience through a unique program that you devise according to your strengths and your needs. These are some suggestions, but you will find others that are helpful as you go along. One thing is sure: the more resilient you become, the less likely it is that you will be overwhelmed when life's challenges come along.

9.

OTHER SOURCES OF HELP

DO I NEED PSYCHOTHERAPY?

Helping yourself is an excellent start and will be necessary whether or not you have a counsellor or a psychiatrist to guide you as you deal with your depression. So, it is not a question of whether you help yourself or see a therapist — you might need to do both. A therapist or counsellor can be a coach and cheerleader for your own efforts, and their support can make a significant difference when you are struggling with a lack of energy and motivation. It helps to know that you are going to report your successes and struggles to someone who is interested in your progress.

In addition, it might be necessary to go deeper. A therapist can help you review parts of your life that have a bearing on the way you are feeling. For some, this may mean for the first time telling their story to someone who really listens. Simple as that sounds, it is a powerful process and provides an opportunity to assess what has happened and be validated. As we grow up, we make decisions about how the world works and where we fit into it. Children are constantly working this out and may, at a very young age, come to conclusions that guide their actions throughout their lives. Children have to resolve questions such as, 'Who can I trust?' 'How competent am I?' 'What happens if I speak my mind?'

Without realizing it, many of us run our lives according to decisions we made when we were very young. A therapist can help you look at those decisions and adapt them to better fit your present situation. Maybe, when you were six, it wasn't safe to speak your mind. Maybe you were punished for it. But as an adult, it might be good to re-evaluate your circumstances. It could be perfectly okay to speak up now but you just haven't tried because that six-year-old says not to.

But if it still isn't safe, maybe you need to change your circle of friends or even your partner. Everyone has the right to be around people who accept and like them. Unlike children, adults can have control over the people they spend time with. Deciding how to create a more positive environment for yourself can be a challenge. Another point of view and some guidance might help here.

So, seeing a counsellor, psychologist or therapist can help in a number of ways. They can coach you as you make changes in your life, listen as you tell your story, or help you to review the guidelines by which you live your life. Most of all, having another human being give you their undivided attention, even for a short time, can be a positive, healing experience in itself.

DO I HAVE AN ADDICTION?

Many people are unaware that the alcohol or other drugs they use socially can have a depressing effect if used frequently. It is tempting to have a few drinks to try to lift yourself out of a down patch, but alcohol is itself a depressant; that's where the relaxing effect comes from. Over time, alcohol and other drug use can contribute significantly to a depression, and it can be a mistake to self-medicate in this way. The temporary relief you might feel masks the fact that there is no lasting improvement.

If you are using these substances as a crutch, talk to your doctor and request an assessment by someone who is experienced in the field of substance abuse. Many people feel that alcohol and cannabis are more 'natural' than antidepressant medication and feel justified in using them as treatment, but they simply do not have the right effect on the brain chemistry. If you would rather use a natural treatment, try some of the natural remedies mentioned later in this chapter (see page 154), combined with the self-care program outlined in Chapter 5. Until depression lets up, it is best to avoid all recreational drugs, including alcohol.

Check out your drinking at **www.alcohol.org.nz** and click on 'Is your drinking okay?' Another useful site is **www. smartrecovery.org** and Alcoholics Anonymous can be found at **www.aa.org**.

DO I NEED MEDICATION?

Many people with depression can be helped by medication. If your depression lasts months rather than weeks, is intensely painful or causes your emotions to feel numb most of the time, or if it includes physiological features such as loss of appetite or disrupted sleep, it may be helpful to talk to your doctor about medication. General practitioners can prescribe antidepressants and/or recommend a consultation with a psychiatrist, who is the specialist in the field of mental health.

There are many antidepressants available and it might take a little trial and error to find the one that suits you best. You can't know for sure whether a particular treatment is working until you try it for a few weeks. Don't be discouraged if the first one doesn't work; there are others that act on different aspects of the brain chemistry.

Side effects can range from a dry mouth and drowsiness to weight gain or loss of sexual response. Often the side effects become less troublesome as you get used to the medication.

Some people feel that there is a stigma attached to taking medication for mental health disorders. The important thing to note is that the medication is designed to adjust the brain's natural supply of serotonin and/or norepinephrine and restore the balance of brain chemistry that helps establish good functioning and a sense of wellbeing.

For some depressed people, it will be just as important to take medication as it is for a diabetic to take insulin — good health cannot be restored without it. The good news is that most people will not need antidepressants for their whole life, though they might be advised to keep taking medication for six months to two years to prevent a relapse.

Choosing whether to take antidepressant medication is a big decision and it's important to take some time to find out what is involved. Ask your doctor about it in detail and read any information sheets you are given. Find out whether there are any side effects and what happens if you drink alcohol or take other drugs or herbal supplements with the medication. In the end, it's your decision.

NATURAL REMEDIES FOR DEPRESSION

Many people turn to herbal remedies and dietary supplements, feeling that they are safer and more natural than pharmacological treatment. While some remedies may have only a placebo effect (which in itself is a kickstart to the healing process), some have been proven through scientific studies to be as effective as conventional medicines.

A systematic review of the research on a number of herbal products found that two products could be proven to be effective in the treatment of anxiety and depression.[1] They are St John's Wort for depression and kava (sometimes known as kava kava) for anxiety. However, it is important to consult your doctor before taking these remedies because they do have side effects and can interact with prescribed medication.

Omega 3 (usually in the form of fish oil but also found in flaxseed oil or obtained by including fish in the diet) has also been proven to have significant benefits in relieving depression in adults and children. Again, care needs to be taken because the benefits are actually reduced at high doses and if fish oils are taken with anticoagulants they may increase the risk of bleeding.

Seasonal affective disorder (SAD) is depression that occurs in the winter months. Light treatment of 30 minutes a day using a specially designed light box with fluorescent white light has been shown to improve symptoms.

Yoga and tai chi have also been shown to have real benefits in health and wellbeing.

Some people find homeopathy effective in the treatment of depression. The medicines used in this process are known as remedies and they are non-toxic, non-habit-forming and do not have side effects. The mechanism of their action is not fully understood, but most homeopaths believe that the homeopathic remedy stimulates the person's own ability to heal.

Homeopathic remedies can be taken at the same time as conventional medication and do not diminish the effectiveness of either treatment. [2]

MEETING YOUR NEEDS

We all have to meet our needs in a variety of ways. Just as we can't live entirely on fish and chips, neither can we be satisfied with a life that is all work or all television. The important thing is to achieve balance in our lives. Meeting our needs and taking good care of ourselves is not just first aid for dealing with a crisis, it's a vital part of a healthy lifestyle that will maintain wellbeing.

Chapter 6 offered one way of looking at our needs. Another is summed up by Rick Hanson when he says that the human animal is primed to do three things: avoid harm, approach rewards and attach to others.[3] Aim to relieve your own suffering in whatever way you can: by good self-care and a non-judgmental attitude towards yourself. Be a good friend to yourself, asking, 'Is this in my best interests?' Look for a balance between pleasure and achievement in the right amounts to give a sense of satisfaction alongside a feeling of peace and relaxation. Understand that close relationships are essential to each of us, and if you don't feel you are receiving love, try to give love to others. Be happy for others' successes and give credit and thanks where they are due. You will warm up your relationships in this way and become a good friend.

Balance all aspects of yourself

Body	Exercise: sport, dancing, gardening, appreciate your physical self and its many skills, observe how useful your hands are, enjoy your strength, nourish your body with healthy food.
Emotions	Let them surface, invite the message they bring: all feelings and emotions are important, you don't have to act on them but you do need to know them.
Social	Do something with other people: join a course or a community group, invite a neighbour in for coffee, call a friend, make a point of talking to someone each day, sit down with your family and ask about their day.
Mind	Join the library, go to a public lecture or talk, read magazines or illustrated books such as travel stories until your concentration improves; be cautious about TV — it can be too passive and often negative in content.
Spirit	Be aware, connect with nature and the world around you through your senses, think about the bigger picture, read about spirituality, join a church or a group that is on your wavelength, connect with friends and family in a compassionate way, show compassion to yourself.

DEALING WITH RELAPSE

Depression might try to make a comeback, but by understanding yourself and embracing a good set of skills you can stop it from taking over. Here are some simple steps to deal with the return of low mood or negative thinking.

Pause

Take a few moments to notice how you are feeling and what thoughts are in your mind. Scan your body and notice any sensations. Become aware of the moment.

Breathe

Take a few slow breaths, attending to each in-breath and out-breath, counting to three as you breathe in, and three as you breathe out. Use the breath to help you to relax.

Make a choice

Based on what you have learnt that works for you, choose something that can help you switch channels: put on a relaxation recording or some enjoyable music, read something that sums up a positive message. Remember, even if the feelings are very strong, they will pass.

Take action

Do whatever you have chosen: something enjoyable or something that gives you a sense of being in control. It could be as small as doing the dishes or tidying your desk, it could be phoning a friend or going for a walk in a favourite place.

HOW IT TURNED OUT

Let's take one last look at the people whose stories we've followed throughout the book.

Laura

When I became pregnant for the second time, I dreaded a return of the depression, but we were watching out for it. I made sure I had a lot of things in place so I could get enough sleep and have some company and help. Things went pretty well. Emma is a great joy to us and Josh loves having a little sister. I can still have the odd day that looks black and I think everything's a mess and my life is a failure

— but I know it for what it is, and I go a bit easy on myself, just putting one foot in front of the other, and usually I wake up the next morning feeling fine. Dave knows when I'm having a bad day and he's a bit more caring, takes the kids for a while when he gets home from work or helps out in some other way. When Emma is old enough for preschool I'll go back to work because I'm not really the housewife type and we'll pay someone to do some of the housework. I hope that I can keep an eye on myself and prevent any other big depressions, but I know now that it's something I'm vulnerable to. I no longer feel guilty about it, and Dave's very understanding, so that helps a lot. I make sure I get a good amount of sleep and I eat well and exercise every day.

Jackson

Things are much better and I'm looking forward to next year, which will be my last year at school. Over the summer I'll look for a job — never thought I would say that without getting sweaty palms! I'm keeping up the exercise and hanging out with a few more mates, so that's all good. I tell them alcohol doesn't suit me and they accept that — they'll be even happier when I get my licence and can be the sober driver.

I've still got that Rainbow Youth card. I googled them and I might check them out ...

Josie

I think I'm a lot stronger for having been through what I did. I understand a lot more than some of my friends, about myself and about how to speak up when it's necessary. Sometimes my friends talk to me about their troubles. I can see when they're not looking after themselves or when they should just talk to their parents and sort things out. Sometimes they try what I suggest and then I'm happy that I've been able to help.

Tom

I'm back on track. The psychologist knows I'll call if I need to but for the past twelve months things have been going smoothly. I'm getting a bit bored with the nursery job and I have a few little business ideas buzzing round in my head, so I might be ready for something new. But first Sally and I are going to Europe for a few weeks. It won't be backpacking but it won't be all shopping either, so we're working on an itinerary with plenty of things we can both enjoy.

Kathy

I understand that depression can be genetic, and I now accept that I will probably need medication throughout my life. Thanks to the combination of medication and psychological help, I see things quite differently now. Maybe at some later date I might be able to come off the medication and my new attitudes might keep me from becoming depressed again. I'll be very cautious about how I do that, though, and I would want to be sure my life was on an even keel.

My husband tackled his depression and for him all the

practical things I had been trying worked without the need for medication. He has a new job that he really enjoys, so that certainly helps. We support each other because we understand what we've each been through. I thought I had been pretty good about hiding my depression from the family, but the children have commented that I'm happier and more fun. They said I didn't laugh and joke with them before. I tell them they're more fun now too!

KEY POINTS
TO REMEMBER

TAKE STOCK

Ask yourself:
- How have I been feeling lately?
- Could I feel better?
- What's going on and what do I need to change?

Take control by putting some structure in your life and attending to your own needs.

TAKE CARE OF YOURSELF PHYSICALLY

Breathe

Maintain an open, tall posture.
- Let your diaphragm do the work.
- Breathe in gently through your nose.
- Check from time to time throughout the day: Am I holding my breath? Can I deepen and slow my breathing?

Relax

- Remember that your body and mind need to rest.
- Observe your thoughts passing like clouds in the sky or cars on the road.
- There are many ways to relax, so choose one that suits you, whether it is listening to a relaxation recording or doing a familiar activity with focused attention.
- Let yourself feel safe.
- Aim to spend 15 minutes every day doing some form of relaxation.

Sleep

Set up a good sleep routine.

- Make sure you are warm and comfortable in bed.
- Reduce caffeine and alcohol intake.
- Avoid screen time for at least an hour before bed.
- Manage worrying thoughts by writing things down to attend to in the morning and thinking of things for which you are grateful.
- Use breathing and relaxation to help you get off to sleep.

Eat well

Use healthy eating to take care of yourself.

- Find out what makes a balanced diet that suits you, making sure it includes protein and plenty of fruit and vegetables for vitamins and minerals.
- Eat at regular meal times and avoid grazing.
- Reduce your sugar intake.

Exercise

We need to move to feel good in ourselves.

- Find an activity you can love — or grow to love — so that you will want to exercise.
- Understand what motivates you: company, competition, peace and quiet.
- Get out into nature if possible.
- There are so many ways to move and enjoy being active, there will be one that suits you.

TAKE CARE OF YOUR THOUGHTS AND FEELINGS

Focus

- Attention is like a flashlight: choose where you would like your beam to shine.
- Thoughts are not facts. Let worries and ruminations float by.
- Keep bringing your focus back to the present, to the task in hand.

Self-talk

- Monitor what is going on in your mind-chatter.
- Take a neutral stance and wait to see how things turn out rather than expecting the worst.
- Do your best then relax about the outcome, accept that what happens, happens.
- Stop self-bullying by suspending judgment on yourself.
- Be supportive of your own efforts — we all do better with encouragement.

Understand what drives your emotions

- Self-protection — recognize our need for safety and the fight/flight/freeze response to threat.
- Manage fear and anger by acknowledging how you feel, identifying the threat and choosing a response.
- Resource-seeking — how we are motivated to achieve. We all need a sense of achievement. Set goals, however small, and give yourself credit for meeting them.
- We are born for love. Seek out good people who support you. Value your friendships.

Manage your emotions

- Put words to your feelings.
- Tolerate your emotions and look for how they can guide you.
- Calm yourself and soothe your emotions — find out what works for you.
- Change the channel — distract yourself from troubling feelings.
- Be patient with yourself and others — everything changes, and bad times pass.
- Cultivate positive feelings.
- Foster a sense of gratefulness.

UNDERSTAND YOUR BELIEFS

- Know where they come from.
- Be prepared to review them from time to time.
- Remember that beliefs provide a map but they are not reality.

CONNECTIONS: YOUR SPIRITUAL LIFE

Values

- Remember that values underpin your life.
- Ask yourself: When do you feel true to yourself? What makes you feel satisfied?
- Check that the parts of life you value most are getting the most of your time and attention.

Mindfulness

- Control your attention (remember the flashlight analogy) and keep coming back to the task in hand.
- Be in the present.
- Slow down.
- Practise regular meditation.

Gratitude

- Remember all the things you have for which you can be grateful.
- Keep a gratitude journal, noting a few things each day for which you are grateful.
- Remember: gratitude encourages hope.

Compassion

- We are all in this together: feel with others.
- Allow your heart to be moved by the suffering of others and yourself.
- Suspend judgment.
- Be kind to yourself.
- Find something or someone to care for.
- Rejoice in others' successes and give credit where it is due.

Creativity
- Make something: a picture, a cake, a garden, a poem; play some music.
- Find the creativity in your work.
- Look for opportunities to enjoy the creativity of others: a movie, an art exhibition, your friend's scrapbook, your child's music.

Relationships
- Depression can be hard on relationships: look outward and greet people.
- Make time for friends and family. Nurture important relationships.
- Share your feelings, your hopes and dreams with someone you trust.
- Repair hurt relationships.
- Forgive and let go of harm done to you.
- Find ways to contribute to your community.

Resilience
- Resilience is like fitness in body, mind and spirit and in our relationships.
- It means having something in reserve to face hard times.
- Paying attention to how you care for yourself and your relationships will help maintain your wellbeing.

ACKNOWLEDGMENTS

Thank you to my colleagues, fellow writers and clients who have shared their wisdom and experience with me and especially to those who gave positive feedback on the first version of this book and encouraged me to take it further.

To Lionel Padial, Lorinda Shaw and Dr Anna Clarkson, who fearlessly critiqued my revisions in the light of their expertise, I am grateful and indebted.

APPENDIX: TABLES

Resilient thinking table

Use the blank table below to help you move your thinking about a
problem from vulnerable to resilient. For an example of how to fill out
the table, see page 77.

Problem	Vulnerable thinking	Resilient thinking
Mental chit-chat (the thoughts that block you or help you)		
Beliefs (What are the underlying beliefs and emotions?)		
Consequences (What will happen if I follow my thoughts?)		

Weekly schedule table

Photocopy the table below and use it to create your own weekly schedule. As with the example on page 67, give each activity a number from 1 to 10 to indicate how much you enjoyed it.

Time	Monday	Tuesday	Wednesday	Thursday	Friday

Time	Monday	Tuesday	Wednesday	Thursday	Friday

BIBLIOGRAPHY

Aldridge, Susan (2000), *Seeing Red and Feeling Blue: A new understanding of mood and emotion*, Arrow, London.

Armstrong, Karen (2011), *Twelve Steps to a Compassionate Life*, The Bodley Head, London.

Gilbert, Paul (1997), *Overcoming Depression: A self-help guide using cognitive-behavioural techniques*, Robinson, London.

Gilbert, Paul (2009), *The Compassionate Mind*, Constable and Robertson, London.

Greenberger, D. and Padesky, C. (1995), *Mind Over Mood: Change how you feel by changing the way you think*, Guilford Press, New York.

Hanson, Rick (2011), *Just One Thing*, New Harbinger, Oakland.

Leonard, George (1992), *Mastery: The keys to success and long-term fulfillment*, Plume, New York.

McKenzie, Stephen and Hassed, Craig (2014), *Mindfulness for Life*, Exisle Publishing, NSW.

Sapolsky, Robert (2002), *A Primate's Memoir: Love, death and baboons in East Africa*, Vintage, New York.

Skellett, Chris (2012), *When Happiness is not Enough*, Exisle Publishing, NSW.

Skellett, Chris (2014), *The Power of the Second Question*, Exisle Publishing, NSW.

Smith, Gwendoline (1995), *Sharing the Load: What to do when someone you love is depressed*, Random House, Auckland.

Solomon, Andrew (2001), *The Noonday Demon: An anatomy of depression*, Chatto and Windus, London.

Williams, Mark and Penman, Danny (2011), *Mindfulness: Finding peace in a frantic world*, Piatkus, London.

Williams, Mark, Teasdale, John, Segal, Zindel and Kabat-Zinn, Jon (2007), *The Mindful Way Through Depression*, Guilford Press, United Kingdom.

ENDNOTES

Chapter 3

1. Huntington's disease is an inherited disease that causes the progressive breakdown (degeneration) of nerve cells in the brain.
2. The Dunedin Multidisciplinary Health and Development Research Unit: http://dunedinstudy.otago.ac.nz/
3. Aldridge, Susan (2000), *Seeing Red and Feeling Blue: A new understanding of mood and emotion*, Arrow, London.
4. Sapolsky, Robert (2002), *A Primate's Memoir: Love, death and baboons in East Africa*, Vintage, New York.
5. Bowlby J. (1969), *Attachment. Attachment and loss, vol. 1. Loss*, Basic Books, New York.
6. Perry, Bruce D. and Szalavitz, Maia (2010), *Born for Love: Why empathy is essential — and endangered*, Harper Collins, New York.
7. Sigmund Freud's *The Psychopathology of Everyday Life* was originally published in the *Monograph for Psychiatry and Neurology* in 1901, before appearing in book form in 1904.

Chapter 4

1. Adler, Alfred (1927), 'The practice and theory of individual psychology' in *The Collected Clinical Works of Alfred Adler*, Alfred Adler Institute of Northwestern Washington.
2. Gilbert, Paul (2009), *The Compassionate Mind*, Constable and Robertson, London.

Chapter 5

1. Dr Edmund Jacobson invented the technique in the 1920s as a way to help his patients deal with anxiety.

2. Mayo Clinic, April 2017: https://www.mayoclinic.org/

3. St-Onge, M.P., Roberts, A., Shechter, A. and Choudhury, A.R. (2015), 'Fiber and saturated fat are associated with sleep arousals and slow wave sleep', *J Clin Sleep Med*, 12(1): 19–24.

4. Julia Rucklidge TEDX article: Rucklidge, Julia J., Kaplan, Bonnie J. and Mulder, Roger T. (2015), 'What if nutrients could treat mental illness?' *Australian and New Zealand Journal of Psychiatry*, 49(5): 1.

5. Bratman, Gregory N., Daily, Gretchen C., Levy, Benjamin J. and Gross, James J. (2015), 'The benefits of nature experience: Improved affect and cognition', *Landscape and Urban Planning*, 138: 41–50.

6. Souter-Brown, Gayle (2017), 'The theoretical basis of well-being as a motivation for design', *Journal of Biourbanism*, 5: 201–18.

Chapter 6

1. Adapted from Carla Shatz's phrase 'Cells that fire together, wire together' and often (mis)quoted. Shatz, Carla J. (1992), 'The Developing Brain, *Scientific American*, 60–7.

2. Doidge, Norman (2007), *The Brain That Changes Itself*, Viking Press, New York and London, p. 427. .

3. Gilbert, Paul (2009), *The Compassionate Mind*, Constable and Robertson, London.

4. Gilbert, Paul (2009).

5. Mischel, Walter, Ebbesen, Ebbe B., Raskoff Zeiss, Antonette (1972). 'Cognitive and attentional mechanisms in delay of gratification', *Journal of Personality and Social Psychology*, 21(2): 204–18.

6. Auckland Writers Festival, May 2015, interviewed by Jim Mora.

7. Ellis, A. and Dryden, W. (1987), *The Practice of Rational Emotive Therapy*, Springer Publishing Company, New York.

Chapter 7

1. Williams, Mark and Penman, Danny (2011), *Mindfulness: Finding peace in a frantic world*, Piatkus, London.
2. Kristen Neff: http://self-compassion.org/the-three-elements-of-self-compassion-2/
3. Murray, Bridget (2002), 'Writing to heal', *Psychology Monitor*, June, 33(6).

Chapter 8

1. Chadwick, Erica (2012), 'Flourishing with savouring strategies', Positive Psychology Symposium, NZ Psychological Society Conference 2012.
2. Rick Hanson: https://www.rickhanson.net/feed-the-mouse/
3. Norberg, Johan (2017), *Progress: Ten reasons to look forward to the future*, Oneworld Publications, London.
4. Smith, Emily Esfahani, 'There's more to life than being happy', TED talk, 26 September 2017.
5. Frankl, Victor (1959), *Man's Search for Meaning*, Beacon Press, Boston.
6. Shakespeare, *Hamlet*, Act II Scene 2.
7. Oettingen, Gabriele (2015), *Rethinking Positive Thinking: Inside the new science of motivation*, Current, London.

Chapter 9

1. Holt, Shaun (2008), *Natural Remedies that Really Work: A New Zealand guide*, Craig Potton Publishing, Nelson.
2. Glaisyer, Mary, RCHom, personal communication 2009.
3. Rick Hanson: http://www.rickhanson.net/love-the-world/

INDEX

Also available in the Empower series ...

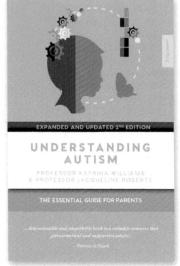

Live and Laugh with Dementia
Lee-Fay Low BSc Psych (Hons), PhD
ISBN 978-1-925335-72-9

Understanding Autism
Prof. Katrina Williams
& Prof. Jacqueline Roberts
ISBN 978-1-925335-71-2

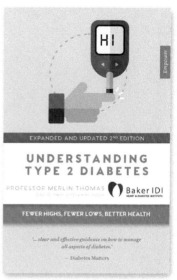

The Digestive Health Solution

Benjamin I. Brown, ND

ISBN 978-1-925335-38-5

Understanding Type 2 Diabetes

Prof. Merlin Thomas

ISBN 978-1-925335-55-2